Wisconsin's AI Leadership Blueprint for 2024

AI Playbook: Real-World Use Cases and Workbook Training for Leaders

Table of Contents

Forward *5*
About Rod Holum JR *6*
About Aaron Libner *8*
The Invisible Threat: How AI Complacency Could Destroy Your Business *10*
How can your small business use AI today? *18*
Demystifying the AI Integration Process *22*
Ethical Considerations and AI in Business *28*
Protecting Artistry in the Digital Age *36*
Taking your first steps with AI: Bing Chat *40*
Using Google Bard/Gemini AI *45*
Exploring Image Generation *51*
Intermediate AI Usage: ChatGPT *55*
Advanced AI Usage: Custom AI with CustomGPT *65*
Driving Non-Profit Efforts with AI *71*

Wisconsin Business Leader Pioneers in AI Interviews

Paul Bagniefski: Leveraging AI in Business *93*
Coach Kowalski Insights: AI in Football and Classroom *97*
Keagan Walz: Harnessing AI's Power in Real Estate *101*
Coach Yash Insights: AI in Everyday Life and Education *105*
Loree Coulthard: HR and Healthcare *107*

4

Forward

In the past years, Artificial Intelligence (AI) has taken the world by storm. It has become the leading buzzword, cropping up in discussions ranging from new software exploration, product development, to investment opportunities.

However, amidst this growing buzz around AI, I've noticed a gap in understanding among many business leaders I interact with. They often lack a basic comprehension of AI, rarely use it in their operations, and are generally uncertain about where to start.

As the CEO of Coulee Tech, my interactions with business leaders across various industries reveal a common thread: a keen interest in leveraging AI's potential coupled with uncertainty about its practical applications. Misconceptions, negative perceptions, and misinformation frequently paint AI more as a figment of science fiction than as a practical tool.

To address this, I've embarked on writing this book and launching a monthly workshop series for leaders. The aim is to enable Wisconsin businesses to effectively embrace AI, offering guidance on integrating it into their operations, and emphasizing the importance of its safe and ethical use.

This book isn't aimed at AI experts. Rather, it's designed for those who seek straightforward, digestible steps to gain a functional understanding of AI for their everyday professional tasks.

About Rod Holum JR

**Author, Speaker, CEO,
Cyber Criminal Butt kicker
AI Advocate for Business**

A computer geek since my teen years in the early '90s, it was a natural progression for me to become a passionate advocate for my clients in AI and cybersecurity.

My IT team is unparalleled in the industry, making it a breeze to rescue clients from substandard IT service. They pride themselves on having calls answered by a live person and offer a $100 guarantee if any voicemail goes unanswered for 59 minutes. **Try them yourself at 608.783.8324 or helpdesk@coulee.tech**

This exceptional team is responsible for my success, leading to our company being listed twice on the Fortune 5000 list of fastest-growing companies, sought-after speaker nationwide and author of multiple books on IT, Cybersecurity and AI.

Most of my time is dedicated to meeting with business leaders, understanding their future goals, and exploring how we can assist them in achieving those objectives.

The Wind in My Sails: My beautiful wife, Laura Holum, and partner of over 20 years, is the cornerstone of my life.

Running a fast-growing, butt-kicking IT and cybersecurity consultancy is demanding, but coming home to a fortress of sanctuary my wife creates is very energizing.

Her fierce love for what matters most - her family – and her sacrificial dedication to them, ensures that we are always well cared for. She has brought three little bundles of joy into our lives, and I am privileged to be raising them into productive adults alongside her.

Our first, Aspen, is preparing to leave the nest next year. She is a clone of my personality, stubborn and passionate. I have no doubt she'll become a formidable leader in any area she dedicated herself to, making me incredibly proud and exhausted at the same time!

Jer and I spend countless nights playing video games and working together on our property, where he enjoys dirt biking, burning stuff, and chopping down trees. He recently completed his first year of high school football as a lineman and is dedicated to his fitness, waking up at 4 am for gym sessions year-round. He is a go getter, and I am sure will end up achieving far more than his father at his current pace!

Our little Ezra is a constant source of happiness, a spitting image of her mother. She adores horse riding and creating miniatures for her tiny houses. Her favorite pastime? Watching movies with Laura!

Our host daughter from Thailand, Nita, is currently thriving in college in La Crosse. She might just love our pets more than us sometimes!

About Aaron Libner

A lifelong friend of CEO Rod Holum Jr, and Chief Acquisition Officer of Coulee Tech, Inc, a leading provider of cybersecurity protection, IT Support, and Software Development, specializing with Healthcare and Manufacturing clients in Wisconsin, Minnesota, and Iowa; headquartered out of La Crosse, WI with a branch Aaron oversees in Eau Claire, WI.

With over 20 year's of sales and leadership experience, Aaron has played an integral role in Coulee Tech's rapid continued growth and doubling of their IT business year after year since April of 2020, when he joined Coulee Tech. Aaron has led as many as 1500 employees over his professional career through sales training, consulting, and sales presentations and seminars. Aaron regularly does presentations to business professionals and organizations on cyber security and the use of AI in business.

Aaron is active in the communities Coulee Tech is in. He is President for a Non-Profit, Fierce Freedom, where they work to end the cycle of human trafficking and exploitation through educational programming that empowers communities and speaks to the worth and dignity of each. He is a Chamber Ambassador for the Eau Claire Area Chamber of Commerce, and advocates for the other 3 Chambers of Commerce Coulee Tech is a part of, La Crosse, Chippewa Falls, and Menomonie. He is a Past President and active Rotarian of the Rotary Club of Eau Claire. He serves on various committees and boards throughout the committee and believes in giving back to the community wholeheartedly.

In 2022, Aaron received the award from the Eau Claire Area Chamber of Commerce for Outstanding Chamber Volunteer of the Year award. Aaron's passion for service started early through scouting and he is also an Eagle Scout in the Boy Scouts of America.

When he is not kicking the butts of cybercriminals, defeating slow computer networks, or writing amazing software solutions, he enjoys spending time his wife, daughter, and family visiting and site seeing various parks, outdoor adventures, and new places around the nation. He and his family are members of Peace Church in Eau Claire, WI. He enjoys family game time, watching movies, and enjoys making memories with friends as well.

Aaron is married to Erin Libner, his life partner and best friend. Erin works at Royal Credit Union (RCU) corporate office as the Member Service and Quality Assurance Specialist. Erin is always kind, thinks of others, and offers to be a helping hand when needed. Aaron and Erin have a 3 going on 4-year-old daughter Raelynn. Raelynn enjoys time with her family, Sunday school at Peace Church, playing in the water or snow, and all the popular kids shows/movies like Paw Patrol or Bluey.

The Invisible Threat: How AI Complacency Could Destroy Your Business

The next few years are moving forward at lightning speed within the AI world and if you sit with your head in the sand in relation to AI your competitors will put you out of business before you even realized they were a threat.

You need two things, to have an IT partner that can help you know where to focus your energy, and to carve out time to explore those areas within your business. If your IT partner isn't talking to you about AI, they are failing you.

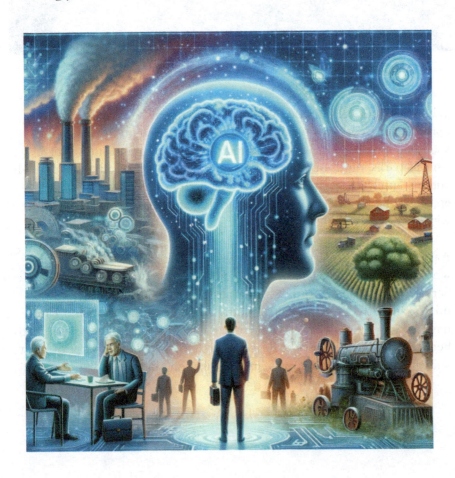

In 1850, roughly 90% of the US economy was built around the growth of food leaving only 10% for non-food production jobs. The industrial revolution drastically changed that to today, in 2024, US food production jobs account for less than 5%. That is an 85% reduction of labor.

If you, fellow reader from the future, told a room of 100 farmers in 1850 that in the future 95 of them will no longer have a farming job within 150 years. What will they do, how will they make a living, how will they feed their family?

The explosion of research careers, executives, counselors, fast food, restaurants, shopping malls, electricians, plumbers, software engineers schools and universities as careers would offer little peace for their fears.

They have seen farming and its safe to them, none of them have seen those professions above and have no idea what that type of world would look like.

As a fellow reader from the future you know the industrial revolution did not create 85% unemployment yet without the foresight of the world would be you lack the ability to combat the fears of those who see the 85% of unneeded farmers.

What it did create is a world and the results of the industrial revolution brought child mortality of children under 5 years old from 30% in 1850 to 3.8% today. Literacy from sub 50% to 86%, death from diseases like chorea, tuberculosis and smallpox to nearly complete eradication worldwide.

Entire books have been written on such improvements because of this. None of which could have happened with those scientists, industrial leaders and teachers who were empowered to pursue those advancements because they were not needed on the farm. That 85% of redirected labor force used it to solve problems plaguing the world to great effect!

This does not ignore the increase in carbon and the likelihood sea levels will rise in a few hundred years, but this book is not a climate crisis book, as others have written far more on that as well.

AI is the next revolution, and it will happen exceptionally quickly. The industrial revolution happened over decades because you needed to physically create machines, foundries, sell and design tractors.

The AI revolution gets deployed at the speed of the internet. You don't need to wait for a factory to be built, that can produce 10 – 20 of the new machines a day. As soon as a new model, new service, new tool is created you can get 100 million users in a month like ChatGPT did. To put in perspective, John Deere, in over 100 years+ has not made 100 million tractors yet.

The Ai that designs your new house, answers all your emails, organizes your schedule, or does any millions of the items you do on a computer is just around the corner and it is either you or your competitor that will start using it first.

As a leader in your business, you need to know how these tools work so you can pivot your business, pivot your staff, and stay ahead of the tsunami of changes coming to your industry.

Wisconsin Business Leader AI Mastermind Workshop

https://www.coulee.tech/ai-mastermind-workshop/

Coulee Tech is hosting a monthly workshop to empower local leaders. The **"Business Leader AI Mastermind Workshop",** an exclusive event designed for business leaders eager to harness the power of artificial intelligence in their organizations.

Held at the vibrant offices of Coulee Tech, Inc. and expanding to Eau Claire and Menomonie in Febuary, this workshop is more than just a learning session; it's a hands-on experience every leader can use that will transform the way you think about and use AI.

What to Expect:
- **Hands-On Learning**: Dive into practical, hands-on lessons tailored for everyday business leaders. Whether you're new to AI or looking to expand your knowledge, our workshop is structured to provide valuable insights for all levels.
- **Exploring New Technologies**: Each session focuses on a new AI technology. Discover cutting-edge tools and learn how they

can be integrated into your business processes for enhanced efficiency and decision-making.
- **Community Knowledge Sharing**: Engage in enriching discussions with your peers about commonly used AI tools. Learn from the collective experiences of the group, gaining insights into what works and what doesn't in real-world scenarios.
- **Live Demonstrations and Projects**: Witness live demos from members showcasing how they've implemented AI in their work. Get inspired by workshop projects and see first-hand the practical applications of AI in various business contexts.

Who Should Attend?
This workshop is ideal for business leaders, managers, entrepreneurs, and anyone interested in leveraging AI to drive business success. Whether you're from a small startup or a large corporation, the insights gained here are invaluable.

Join Us
Elevate your business acumen with AI. Our workshop is a unique opportunity to network, learn, and grow with like-minded professionals. Dates for our upcoming sessions are to be determined, but we encourage you to express your interest early.

The Dawn of AI: Theory Meets Computation

The seeds of AI were sown in the early to mid-20th century, where groundbreaking work by the likes of Alan Turing laid the theoretical foundations. Turing introduced the concept of a machine that could simulate any human intelligence, which he called the "Universal Turing Machine." This idea was a harbinger of things to come.

By the 1950s and 1960s, the term "artificial intelligence" was coined, and the field started gaining traction. Early researchers and pioneers like John McCarthy, Marvin Minsky, and Allen Newell believed that machines could be designed to mimic cognitive functions such as learning and problem solving. This era gave birth to the first chess-playing programs, basic natural language processors, and the fundamental principles of AI.

1970s-1990s: Winter and Revival
AI went through its first "winter" in the 1970s due to inflated expectations and the challenges of scaling up. Funding dried up, and skepticism grew. However, as we moved into the 1980s, there was a resurgence of interest driven by the adoption of "expert systems" — computer programs that mimic the decision-making abilities of a human expert.

The 1990s introduced significant progress. Machine learning, a subset of AI focusing on the idea that systems can automatically learn and improve from experience, began to flourish. Algorithms like backpropagation allowed computers to adjust their internal parameters in response to errors, making learning more efficient.

2000s: The Playground of Tech Titans

The 21st century saw the rise of the internet and a massive influx of data. Tech giants like Google, Facebook, and Amazon started leveraging AI to sift through this vast ocean of information. They developed algorithms that could recommend products, optimize search results, and even recognize faces in photos. For a while, AI seemed like the exclusive domain of these behemoths, given the immense computational power and data they commanded.

Machine learning grew more sophisticated, and a subfield called "deep learning," inspired by the structure and function of the brain, came to the fore. Neural networks, with their ability to process vast amounts of information, became instrumental in significant AI breakthroughs. The challenge, however, was that these algorithms required vast computational resources — often only accessible to large companies with deep pockets.

2010s and Beyond: Democratization of AI

While the early 2000s painted a picture of AI as the stronghold of tech giants, the narrative started to shift by the 2010s. A combination of factors facilitated this:

Open Source Movement: Many AI frameworks and tools, like TensorFlow and PyTorch, became open-source. This made state-of-the-art AI models and algorithms accessible to anyone with an interest. Cloud Computing: Companies like Amazon, Microsoft, and Google began offering AI capabilities as cloud services. This meant that small businesses didn't need to invest in expensive hardware; they could rent computational power as needed.

Pre-trained Models: Instead of training models from scratch, developers could use pre-trained models and fine-tune them for specific tasks, drastically reducing the time, data, and resources required.

SaaS AI Products: Numerous platforms began offering Software-as-a-Service (SaaS) products embedded with AI capabilities, from CRM systems to marketing automation tools.

Knowledge Sharing: Online platforms, courses, and communities proliferated, democratizing knowledge around AI and enabling even those without a deep tech background to grasp its fundamentals.

AI in the Hands of Small Businesses

The implications of these changes were profound for small businesses. What was once a distant, almost mythical tool of the big players, AI became a practical, accessible solution for everyday challenges:

- Local retailers started using AI-driven analytics to forecast sales.
- Small clinics implemented AI tools to assist with patient record analysis.
- Boutique marketing agencies leveraged AI to optimize ad campaigns in real-time.

In essence, AI transitioned from being a luxury to a necessity. No longer the exclusive domain of Silicon Valley's giants, it became an integral tool for businesses of all sizes, helping level the playing field in an increasingly competitive digital landscape. The message was clear: in the modern era, AI isn't just for the big players; it's for everyone.

How can your small business use AI today?

If you run a small 10-person company or are a department lead at a large enterprise, there are multiple ways to incorporate AI without requiring a dedicated tech team or massive financial investment.

We will go in depth later in this book on the "hows" of deploying each of these solutions. Some can give you useful time saving features in minutes, others might take some setup and training.

Here are some user-friendly avenues for such businesses to start harnessing the power of AI:

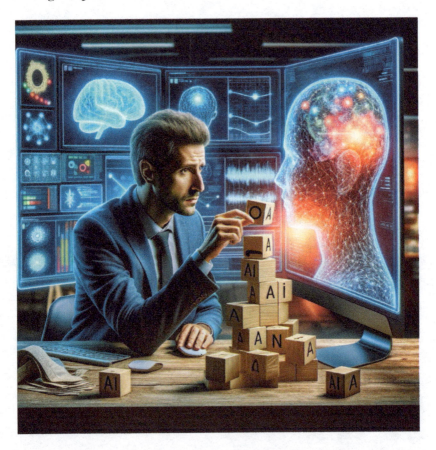

1. **Customer Support with Chatbots:**
   - **What it does:** Provides instant responses to frequently asked customer questions.
   - **Implementation:** Many platforms, such as Intercom, Drift, or Tidio, offer easy-to-set-up chatbots. They can be integrated into your website, allowing for improved customer service and freeing up your team from handling routine queries.

2. **Email Marketing Optimization:**
   - **What it does:** Improves email open rates and engagement through AI-driven content recommendations and send-time optimizations.
   - **Implementation:** Platforms like Mailchimp and HubSpot use AI to suggest the best times to send emails based on your audience's past behavior.

3. **Sales Predictions and Lead Scoring:**
   - **What it does:** Prioritizes potential leads based on how likely they are to convert, helping your sales team focus on the most promising opportunities.
   - **Implementation:** CRM systems like Salesforce and Zoho offer AI features that score leads based on data and past interactions.

4. **Content Recommendations:**
   - **What it does:** Offers personalized content or product recommendations to website visitors, enhancing user experience and increasing sales.
   - **Implementation:** Platforms like Optimizely or Dynamic Yield allow for AI-driven content personalization based on user behavior.

5. **Social Media Insights:**
   - **What it does:** Analyzes social media data to derive insights about audience engagement, sentiment, and trending topics.
   - **Implementation:** Tools like Hootsuite and Buffer offer AI-driven insights to help improve your social media strategy.

6. **Automated Bookkeeping:**
   - **What it does:** Categorizes expenses, tracks invoices, and provides financial insights.

- **Implementation:** Accounting software like QuickBooks and Xero use AI to automate many bookkeeping tasks, reducing the manual effort required.

7. **HR and Recruitment:**
   - **What it does:** Screens resumes, schedules interviews, and even evaluates candidate fit based on predefined criteria.
   - **Implementation:** Platforms like Pymetrics and Harver allow businesses to streamline the recruitment process through AI-driven assessments.

8. **Voice Assistants for Task Management:**
   - **What it does:** Helps with scheduling, reminders, and even basic research or data retrieval.
   - **Implementation:** Integrating tools like Amazon's Alexa or Google Assistant into your workplace can automate basic tasks.

9. **Inventory and Supply Chain Management:**
   - **What it does:** Predicts stock requirements, optimizes inventory levels, and even suggests pricing strategies.
   - **Implementation:** Systems like Shopify for e-commerce use AI to provide insights on inventory management and sales predictions.

10. **Document and Contract Analysis:**
    - **What it does:** Scans documents for key terms, analyzes contract clauses, and even suggests changes.
    - **Implementation:** Tools like Kira, ThoughtRiver, or Contract Mill can help businesses, especially those dealing with numerous contracts or legal documents, streamline their processes.

For small companies, the key is to start with one or two AI applications that directly address specific pain points or areas of potential growth. As familiarity with these tools grows, the company can explore further integrations, gradually expanding the role of AI in their operations.

Demystifying the AI Integration Process

2013 my cofounder and brother graduated from some courses at Stanford University on AI development. It was exceptionally interesting however not applicable with our clients at the time.

A few years later my interest was piqued by a rudimentary AI capable of generating 200-character text responses—roughly 30 words—in reply to queries and answering simple questions. This was early 2019 and while it wasn't earth shattering and its context were close to that of a high school student, seeing the progression from 2013 to 2019 proved to me this was the future as it isn't about where it is today, but where it will be next year.

The lockdowns of 2020 provided an opportunity for deeper exploration. I engaged with fellow peers, sharing my growing passion for AI and annoying anyone who would listen to me about it.

By 2021, my personal exploration had sparked interest from industry colleagues, leading to an invitation to speak at a cybersecurity conference in Nashville, TN addressing 400 Cyber Security CEOs on how they could use AI.

At that time, AI was less sophisticated than today, but its potential was evident. I had the chance to meet notable figures like George Foreman and Damon John from Shark Tank, discussing the impending AI revolution.

In January 2023, my earlier predictions about AI began to materialize. Being re-invited to an industry peer event in San Diego to give an updated speech to the group about AI's evolution from performing basic tasks to emulating intricate computer systems and providing intelligent responses to almost any question.

A love for learning and speaking has opened many doors and I believe the more business leaders experience AI, they will see it as a valuable, critical tool for their success and not an enemy to be feared which is why I take almost any speaking opportunity I can to advocate for the use of AI in business!

Overcoming Common Misconceptions

When many hear "AI", it conjures images of robots taking over jobs or complex algorithms comprehensible only to tech whizzes. We see terminators long before we see wall-e.

The narrative surrounding AI often revolves around the fear of it replacing human jobs. Let's step back and draw a parallel from history.

Some of my readers remember a workplace devoid of computers and the trepidation when computers made their grand entrance into workplaces. Many feared they would make typewriters obsolete and render typists jobless. Yet, what truly transpired was a transition rather than termination. Typists evolved into computer operators. The tool changed, but the essence of the job — processing information efficiently — remained intact.

AI isn't about replacing humans; it's about augmentation. It's about providing businesses and individuals with the tools to carry out repetitive tasks more efficiently, allowing humans to zero in on areas where they truly shine — creativity, empathy, and strategic thinking.

AI won't take your job. Those using AI will

A fitting example of this augmentation is when we worked closely with a non-profit organization. The president of their board was tasked with writing grants — a critical yet time-consuming endeavor. By introducing him to AI-powered tools, we were able to streamline parts of the grant writing process.

The AI tool provided suggestions, outlined structures, and highlighted key points to be included. With this aid, the president could focus more on the organization's narrative and goals rather than getting bogged down by the technicalities. This not only made the grant application process more efficient but also more effective, increasing the chances of securing funds.

In our fast-paced, ever-evolving business environment, standing still is not an option. Embracing change, especially technological advancements like AI, isn't just smart — it's essential. Ignoring this wave of innovation might leave one trailing in the wake of competitors.

However, adopting and integrating AI means not just keeping pace with competitors but often outpacing them. AI is not a threat; it's an opportunity. An opportunity to enhance our capabilities, refine our strategies, and solidify our place as innovators.

You don't need to be a tech behemoth with endless resources to leverage the potential of AI.

As an MSP firm, we've witnessed firsthand the transformative impact of AI on businesses, regardless of their size or domain. It's a game-changer, enabling businesses to transcend traditional boundaries, bolster efficiency, and deliver unparalleled value to their clientele.

Today, the market is ripe with AI tools designed specifically for small to medium-sized businesses. These tools are user-friendly and often plug-and-play, meaning minimal setup time and immediate results. From AI-driven customer relationship management systems that anticipate client needs to AI-based accounting tools that can forecast financial trends, the possibilities are vast and varied.

Employees benefit too. AI can shoulder many of the repetitive tasks that often bog down staff, freeing them to focus on more valuable and fulfilling aspects of their roles. Imagine a customer service rep assisted by an AI chatbot, handling multiple queries simultaneously, reducing wait times, and ensuring customer satisfaction. Or consider a marketing executive using AI-powered analytics to pinpoint the most effective channels for campaigns, eliminating the guesswork and enhancing the ROI or simply creating engaging social media posts.

Moreover, with AI's intuitive learning capabilities, even employees without advanced degrees can handle complex tasks. A store manager without a background in data science can utilize AI-driven insights to optimize stock levels. An HR executive, armed with AI tools, can predict talent trends and streamline recruitment processes, ensuring the right talent is onboarded at the right time.

But it's not just about efficiency; it's about reducing the inherent stress associated with manual, repetitive tasks. By letting AI handle the mundane, employees can breathe easier, focusing on innovation, relationship-building, and strategic planning.

In essence, AI democratizes access to cutting-edge capabilities. No longer is advanced AI tech the sole domain of Silicon Valley giants. Today, even a local store in La Crosse or a budding enterprise in Eau Claire can harness the might of AI, ensuring they remain competitive, relevant, and ready for the challenges of tomorrow.

Assessing the Need for AI in Your Business

The adoption of AI should never be about jumping onto a trendy bandwagon. Rather, it's about understanding its potential to address real business needs. As businesses in the heart of Wisconsin experience the digital evolution, questions arise: How does one decide when and where to incorporate AI? Begin by examining:

1. **Identifying Bottlenecks**: Where does my business encounter obstacles or inefficiencies? It could be anything from handling customer queries, managing inventory, forecasting sales, or enhancing marketing outreach. AI's strength lies in optimizing processes where traditional methods might not be adequate.

2. **Data Utilization**: AI thrives on data. The question is, do you have it? Even what might seem mundane — customer feedback, sales records, website visits — can become a goldmine when processed by AI. The insights drawn can revolutionize decision-making.

3. **Cost-Benefit Analysis**: Every business decision involves weighing costs against potential benefits. While there's an investment associated with AI integration, it's crucial to consider the long-term dividends. Enhanced efficiency, increased sales, improved customer experience – the potential ROI can be manifold.

In the lively business hubs of Wisconsin, AI is more than just a fancy term or a trendy concept from Silicon Valley. It's a real and powerful force, changing the way companies operate and compete.

Our work with various clients in La Crosse and Eau Claire has shown that AI is useful for everyone. It doesn't matter if you run a charity, a local shop, or a manufacturer – there's an AI solution out there for you.

To integrate AI, you need to understand its details, see its potential, and use its strengths to meet your business goals. We're with you every step of the way on this journey, helping to light your path and make the transition smoother.

Ethical Considerations and AI in Business

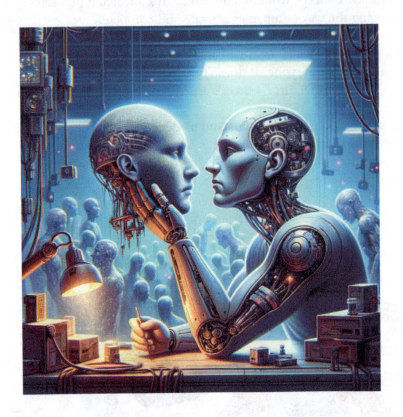

In the mosaic of AI's transformative potential, there's a crucial piece that businesses, especially in the tight-knit communities of Wisconsin and Minnesota, must never overlook ethics. The fusion of technology and morality is not just about compliance or public relations. It's about establishing a foundation of trust.

In the rapidly evolving world of AI. At the heart of this intersection is a tug-of-war between the potential societal benefits of AI-driven solutions and the inviolable rights of the individual. The stakes are incredibly high: on one side, the promise of breakthroughs that can save countless lives; on the other, the sanctity of personal data and the risks associated with its misuse.

To truly understand the depth and nuance of this debate, consider the perspectives of two individuals, both shaped by their unique experiences and worldviews. Their stories underscore that ethical considerations in AI aren't just academic or theoretical—they're deeply personal, rooted in real-life experiences and values.

Scenario: AI-driven Health Research Using Personal Medical Data

A leading healthcare organization has developed an AI tool that analyzes medical records to identify patterns and potential cures for life-threatening diseases. The tool requires a vast amount of patient data to be effective. Without sufficient data, its predictive capabilities are impossible, making the discovery of a cure out of reach.

Person A's Perspective:

Worldview: Person A has seen the devastating effects of this disease up close especially in underserved communities and nations. They deeply value advancements in medical research and believe that every possible effort should be made to empower underserved communities with low cost diagnostic tools for life saving measures.

Ethical Interpretation: From Person A's perspective, using medical data for this purpose is not only ethical but also imperative. The potential to save countless lives outweighs the risks associated with data privacy and it would be unethical not to pursue this. They argue that in the grand scheme of things, the common good should take precedence.

Person B's Perspective:

Worldview: Having emigrated from an authoritarian country, Person B has witnessed firsthand the misuse of personal data by authorities to suppress, control, and harm citizens. This experience has fostered a deep-seated mistrust in any entity having access to personal information. As a result, they fiercely prioritize personal freedom and the right to privacy, viewing it as a safeguard against potential oppression and misuse of power.

Ethical Interpretation: To Person B, using medical data without explicit, informed consent is deeply troubling and reminiscent of the surveillance and control they escaped from. They argue that data collection should always be voluntary, regardless of the potential broader societal benefits. From their perspective, the potential misuse and abuse of such data could have dire consequences and end in more lives lost than any potential benefits.

I am sure you are reading this, your hope is that these two people don't show up at your thanksgiving dinner table or family gathering. Not because you necessarily agree or disagree, but a discussion between them will result in passionate discussion.

Here, the ethical quandary centers around the balance between collective benefits and individual privacy. Your ethical world view might be somewhere in between these two but as the world of AI advances, the ethical debate is going on. AI challenges the status quo invoking fear, excitement, visions of a utopia and of the end of the world all in the same paragraph.

Their fundamental beliefs and values shape their ethical judgments. This divergence highlights the importance of open dialogue and consideration when determining the ethical boundaries of technologies, especially as influential as AI but a reminder as well that two people could both be right and not agree while simultaneously believing the other is wrong.

Ethics in the Age of AI: Universality vs. Personal Convictions

In our multifaceted world, the lines between universal ethical principles and personal opinions often blur. Ethics, at its essence, revolves around the discernment of right from wrong, serving as a guiding compass of our decisions and actions. While laws lay down the boundaries of permissible conduct, ethics often ventures into the gray zones, delineating our moral obligations. However, what complicates this arena further is the presumption by many that their personal ethical beliefs should be universally acknowledged and adhered to.

Differentiating Ethics from Opinion

1. **Origin:**
    - Ethics: Springs from collective values, societal conventions, or philosophical thought. It establishes a commonly accepted yardstick for what's deemed appropriate.
    - Opinion: Anchored in individual experiences, sentiments, and insights, which may differ extensively from one person to the next.

2. **Scope:**
    - Ethics: Generally commands a more universal consensus. For instance, the virtue of honesty is esteemed across diverse cultures and communities.
    - Opinion: Is inherently subjective. A viewpoint held strongly by one might be completely contrary to another's.

3. **Constancy:**
    - Ethics: While it typically remains stable over durations, profound societal changes can redefine ethical standards.
    - Opinion: Fluid by nature, it can evolve with new experiences, enlightenment, or personal progression.

In the unfolding narrative of AI, the interplay between ethics and opinion takes center stage. While this isn't a treatise on ethics, it's pivotal to establish a framework as we navigate this intricate topic. Our objective isn't to find definitive answers but to better comprehend the questions and concerns surrounding AI's ethical implications. The majority's perception doesn't automatically bestow ethical righteousness.

Ethical Framework: Guiding AI with Professional Standards

In every professional realm, the line between right and wrong isn't always crystal clear. As AI continues to evolve, intertwining itself with various industries, the ethical concerns surrounding its usage become increasingly nuanced. Navigating these complexities requires a guiding light, and often, the most illuminating path is the ethical framework established by industry standards.

Why Rely on Industry Ethical Frameworks?

1. **Tried and Tested**: These frameworks aren't conjured overnight. They evolve from years, even decades, of professional experiences, mistakes, and lessons learned. They represent a cumulative wisdom, offering a practical guide to tackling real-world dilemmas.

2. **Consistency in Decision Making**: By adhering to industry-specific ethical frameworks, organizations can ensure consistent decision-making. It reduces the variability that comes from individual opinions and biases.

3. **Legitimacy and Trust**: Aligning AI decisions with established industry ethics enhances the credibility of the organization. Stakeholders, clients, and the public are more likely to trust an entity that operates within recognized ethical bounds.

4. **Provides Clarity**: Ethical ambiguities can be paralyzing. By using a predefined ethical framework, organizations can swiftly determine the best course of action.

Implementing Ethical Frameworks in AI Decisions:

1. **Identification**: Begin by identifying the ethical frameworks or standards relevant to your industry. For instance, the medical profession has the Hippocratic Oath, while journalists adhere to principles of truth and accuracy.

2. **Integration with AI Systems**: Once the relevant ethical principles are identified, they need to be integrated into the AI's decision-making processes. This may involve coding certain hard boundaries or guiding principles into the AI system.

3. **Continuous Review**: The world of AI is rapidly evolving, as are industry standards. It's vital to periodically review and update the ethical guidelines the AI systems follow to ensure they remain current.

4. **Stakeholder Involvement**: It's essential to involve various stakeholders, including employees, clients, and even the public, in discussions about the ethical use of AI. This ensures a holistic and inclusive approach.

While individual opinions on ethics can vary widely, industry standards offer a more universally accepted gauge of what's ethics your industry should follow. As AI becomes an indispensable tool across professions, anchoring its usage in industry-specific ethical frameworks ensures not only its effective application but also a collective yard stick to measure its ethical usage by. In regions like Wisconsin and Minnesota, where community and trust are at the forefront, adhering to these ethical benchmarks in AI practices is not just ideal—it's fundamental.

Understanding AI Bias:
Artificial Intelligence, while revered for its computational prowess, can still inherit and magnify human biases if its training data is unbalanced. Developers are constantly refining AI models to counteract these biases by using more representative and diverse data sets. However, as these improvements are ongoing, everyday users have a role to play in ensuring the ethical use of AI tools.

Tips for Everyday Users to Navigate AI Bias:
1. **Engineer Your Prompt for Diversity**: When using AI tools, be mindful of your phrasing. Requesting diverse perspectives or examples can yield more balanced results. For instance, when seeking historical insights, you might ask, "Provide examples of influential figures from various cultures and genders."

2. **Review and Reroll**: Scrutinize AI-generated content for potential biases. If an output seems skewed, rerun your request or prompt the AI for a broader perspective.

3. **Refine Your Requests**: To receive more nuanced answers, be specific in your prompts. Instead of querying, "Who are notable leaders?", you could ask, "Can you list pioneering leaders from both male and female backgrounds?"

By actively practicing these steps, users can harness the potential of AI while also encouraging a landscape of inclusivity and awareness.

Here are some examples of how you can engineer prompts to counteract or minimize various common biases:

1. **Gender Bias**:
    - Biased Prompt: "Who are the world's greatest scientists?"
    - Counteract Bias: "Provide examples of prominent male and female scientists across history."
2. **Cultural Bias**:
    - Biased Prompt: "Tell me about traditional music."
    - Counteract Bias: "Describe traditional music from African, European, Asian, and South American cultures."
3. **Age Bias**:
    - Biased Prompt: "Who are the tech industry leaders?"
    - Counteract Bias: "Can you list tech industry leaders from both older and younger generations?"
4. **Socioeconomic Bias**:
    - Biased Prompt: "What are popular hobbies?"
    - Counteract Bias: "Describe hobbies enjoyed by people across various socioeconomic backgrounds."
5. **Ability Bias**:
    - Biased Prompt: "What are common ways people commute to work?"
    - Counteract Bias: "List commuting methods suitable for both able-bodied individuals and those with physical disabilities."
6. **Geographical Bias**:
    - Biased Prompt: "Name renowned universities."

- Counteract Bias: "Name top universities from North America, Africa, Asia, Europe, and Australia."

By deliberately engineering prompts in such a manner, users can ensure a broader, more inclusive perspective in the AI's responses while AI makers create greater inclusion in their training data sets. This approach not only minimizes biases but also educates and enriches the user with diverse information.

Protecting Artistry in the Digital Age: Navigating Copyrights and AI Training

The idea that AI should not be trained on copyrighted works without the explicit consent of the original creators resonates with many. Such unauthorized usage can be perceived as undermining the rights of artists and writers, bypassing the core value of acknowledging and compensating creativity. One might argue that if it's unacceptable to reproduce a book or song without proper permissions, then surely AI shouldn't exploit such creative works either. This sentiment, while seemingly straightforward, gets complex when adjacent against legal precedents.

The U.S. Patent and Trademark Office (USPTO) grappled with a similar moral quandary. In 1976, with the Copyright Act, the concept of "Fair Use" was codified to strike a balance between the rights of creators and the broader public interest. The essence of Fair Use is to foster learning, encourage creativity, and safeguard freedom of expression by delineating a middle ground between copyright holders, including both individual artists and large corporations.

Imagine a hypothetical: Rodney Holum copyrights his name while running for president. Without Fair Use, if a news outlet were to pen an unfavorable article using his copyrighted name, he could potentially sue them for copyright infringement. Such a scenario gives one of a thousand examples of the vital role of Fair Use, ensuring that expressions like names and slogans can be used for purposes like reporting.

Fast forward to 2019: OpenAI approached the USPTO, seeking clarity on whether Fair Use could extend to AI training. Given that the doctrine of Fair Use was designed to stimulate learning, innovation, and free expression, the USPTO determined that training AIs on copyrighted material was permissible, provided the copyrighted content isn't present in the final model.

Consequently, within the U.S., AI models can legally train on a vast array of content, from films and books to artworks. The unintended consequence of the 1976 Copyright Act, in tandem with the 2019 USPTO decision, signifies that this practice will likely persist.

But does legality equate to ethicality? The answer might vary depending on the ethical framework your profession adheres to and how it is written. However, in terms of legality, the matter was conclusively settled in favor of AI training years ago.

Data Privacy and Protection:

With great data comes great responsibility. As businesses leverage vast amounts of data to fuel their AI systems, they must also prioritize protecting that data.

Consent is Key: Before collecting or processing data, especially personal data, ensure that you have informed consent. Transparency about how data will be used can build trust with customers.

Encryption and Security: It's not enough to just collect data; it's essential to protect it. Using state-of-the-art encryption methods and constantly updating security protocols can safeguard data from breaches. New laws like the FTC Safeguard which went into effect June 2023 put legal obligation on most businesses that collect any customer information.

Ethical Use of AI-driven Tools:

The power of AI can be intoxicating. But with that power comes a responsibility to use it ethically.

Transparency: Especially in a world where AI decisions can significantly impact individuals' lives, be it in healthcare, finance, or employment. Stakeholders have a right to understand how these decisions are made.

Human-in-the-Loop: AI should complement human decision-making, not replace it. Having a human in the loop can ensure that AI doesn't operate in a vacuum and that decisions taken are always in the best interest of all stakeholders.

In the evolving landscape of AI in business, walking the ethical tightrope can be challenging. Yet, it's a non-negotiable aspect of responsible AI adoption. As businesses in La Crosse, Eau Claire, and beyond venture deeper into the AI realm, they carry the torch of ensuring that technology remains a force for good, underpinned by values that resonate with the communities they serve.

Taking your first steps with AI: Bing Chat

Embarking on a new discipline or learning, especially in the dynamic world of Artificial Intelligence, begins with a fundamental step. This section is designed to guide you, particularly if you're new to AI and haven't invested in any premium services yet.

Our primary focus will be on Bing Chat, which, at the time of this writing, is accessible at https://Bing.com/chat and you must use **Microsoft EDGE**. We're also anticipating a significant shift, with Microsoft planning to integrate Bing Chat into Co-Pilot. Given the rapid evolution in this field, you might need to perform a quick search to catch up with the latest developments and branding changes.

Additionally, we'll delve into Google Bard and ChatGPT 3.5 — the latter being the latest free version available as of now. I've dedicated a whole chapter to ChatGPT, where you'll find practical examples based on version 3.5.

One key advantage of Bing Chat is that it's a cost-free resource, offering real-time, relevant information that can be incredibly valuable for practical applications.

Given it's November 2023, let's put Bing to the test: Can it assist in meticulously planning a weekend in Madison two to three months from now? If you're following along in real-time, adjust your planning timeline accordingly to about two months ahead.

Prompt: *I am going to Madison in January. What are some things I could do?*

Bings Response:
Madison, Wisconsin, offers a variety of activities in January. Here are some suggestions:

1. Witness the massive Wisconsin State Capitol Holiday Tree: **Each year, a balsam fir tree grown in Wisconsin graces the Capitol rotunda**[1].
2. Get out on the frozen lakes: Madison's five lakes are a year-round playground. **You can step right on any of the lakes from anywhere and walk, dance, sip coffee, ice fish or take in all the beauty of Madison**[1].
3. Follow Olbrich's Holiday Express: **Large-scale model trains wind through a holiday scene overflowing with hundreds of poinsettias and fresh evergreens at Olbrich Botanical Gardens**[1].
4. Tap into the craft beverage scene: **Hop on to the Madison On Tap Craft Beverage Trail to earn prizes, get discounts and taste what Madison is all about**[1].
5. Have a meal where dinner is also the show: **Get a front-row seat to one of the best meals of your life at Delectable**[1].
6. Ice skate at The Edgewater: **This 4,000-square-foot rink is a Madison favorite for friends, family and the occasional marriage proposal**[1].
7. Ooh and ahh at holiday light displays: **A beloved holiday tradition, Holiday Fantasy in Lights, has been lighting Madison's Olin Park—and warming our hearts—for 30 years**[1].
8. Try a new winter sport: **Ice skating, snow shoeing, skiing and more are all available in the Greater Madison area**[1].
9. Dine out in a dome: **Be enthralled in a tiny winter wonderland while enjoying a great meal, a beer or cheese board**[1].

Remember to check the local guidelines and restrictions due to COVID-19 before planning your visit. Enjoy your trip! □

Hard to see in a book, but each of these come with a link I could click on to learn more. Lets dive into one of these items. If you customized your search, ask how to do one of the items on your list.

Prompt: *How much is dine out in a dome and what is required to make that happen?*

Bing Response:
Dining in a dome in Madison offers a unique and cozy experience. Here are some options:

1. **Café Hollander**: The heated Dutch domes at Café Hollander provide a cozy oasis. Your reservation includes 90 minutes in a private, heated dome, with

seating for up to eight and a drink package of your choice. **The cost is $75 on weekdays or $100 on weekends**[1].

2. **Karben4 Brewing**: They offer five different experiences — four distinctly themed igloo rentals and a firepit space. **Pricing varies for weekday and weekend rentals**[1].
3. **Nineteen09**: For $75, you can bring up to eight guests for a two-hour visit. **A menu of drinks and snacks including hot beverages, charcuterie, cocktail packages, beer and seltzer buckets, mocktail pitchers and wine are available for purchase**[1].
4. **The Lone Girl Brewing Company**: Rent a cozy dome with up to 10 people for 90 minutes. **You can order off the full menu and choose specialty add-on packages like a hot cocoa bar, mimosa bar or champagne toast**[1].
5. Iron Amethyst Inn: **A 90-minute reservation comes with a charcuterie board, appetizers and drink tickets**[1].

Reservations can fill up fast, so it's recommended to book your spot in advance[1]. Enjoy your dining experience! ☐

Lets get some details on booking Karben4 Brewing!

Prompt: Can I have details on booking Karben4 Brewing

Bing Chat:
Karben4 Brewing in Madison, WI offers a unique winter patio experience with four different igloo experiences, a gas fire pit, and three wood fire pits[1]. Here are some details:

- Location: 3698 Kinsman Boulevard, Madison, WI 53704[1].
- Contact: +1 608-241-4811[1].
- Hours: Today 12:00 PM – 6:00 PM[1].
- Booking: You can book your igloo experience through their website[1].
- Food: This year, Karben4 is excited to host Paddy's Patties. **Their house-made smash burgers and French fries are available to order directly from your igloo**[1]. They also have a variety of personal-sized frozen pizzas from Salvatore's Tomato Pies, soft pretzels from Batch Bakehouse, and a rotating selection of small, locally sourced snacks available for purchase[1].
- Beverages: You will be able to order beverages and Karben4 snacks contactless from your igloo[1].
- Capacity: Each igloo can accommodate up to 8 adult humans comfortably[1].

Please note that smoking and pets are not allowed in the igloos[1]. Enjoy your experience at Karben4 Brewing! ☐

If you are like me, and have a horrible time trying to think of things to do with your significant other, or are not great at planning. This AI could save your marriage! In less than 5 minutes I was able to find a unique experience my wife would love. You could run this type of search any time you are going to go out of town.

Take some time and try your own searches. Think of a place you are going to go and ask it for some events or items. Try:

1. *I am going to <name of city>, what is a good hotel to stay in.*
    a. I tried a small town, Rice Lake, WI and Bing chat found my hotel I stay in when I travel that way. Try your favorite small town and see what it finds!
2. *I am going to take a client out for a fancy meal next weekend in <city name>, where should I go?*
    a. I tried Eau Claire and it gave a number of great suggestions!
3. *I am driving from La Crosse WI to Indianapolis, IN could you plan my trip so I can stop every 2 – 3 hours?*
    a. With your test, change the cities to a trip you take often.
    b. After you get suggestions, you could ask for items like, could you give me an address to go to for free parking, or what food options are available.

A unique use case I worked with one of my medical clients on was helping patients in recovery stay up with their peer groups while traveling. Someone struggling with a drug or substance abuse addiction has a significantly higher chance of success with recovery if he/she stays in support.

4. *I will be driving from Eau Claire to Chicago, Il tomorrow, could you give me a list of AA meetings along the way I could stop by? I leave at 8 am*

Other great prompts:
5. What is the latest news on the stock market?
6. Tell me about the latest advancements in AI technology.
7. What are the best cities to start a tech company?
    a. Change the name to your industry, and/or a state you live in that might be good for expansion of your products.
8. What are the best practices for remote team management?
9. What are the key takeaways from the latest World Economic Forum?
10. What are the latest cybersecurity threats businesses should be aware of?

a. Hint, Call Coulee Tech at 608.783.8324 to help protect you, I am sure the AI would say to do and not just because that is where this author works.
11. I have an employee who has a medical condition which makes them unable to perform their job. We have tried reasonable accommodations, but their performance is still substandard. I am an HR specialist and want to double check my understanding with an AI. What would you recommend?
12. Who are the top competitors of Tesla
    a. Change the name of Tesla to your company, or even a competitor.
13. We are a small company, 15 employees and looking for a good online accounting software. What would you recommend?
    a. Use this method to get any recommendations on software, be it ERP, MRP, Scheduling, 3d modeling or EMR. If you don't know an acronym I used, you probably don't need that type of software.
14. A book I read used the acronym EMR related to software. What would that be?
15. I am meeting a client from a Medical clinic that specializes in Behavioral Health Counseling. Could you explain to me what they do and how I might connect with them as I sell insurance? Could you give me a few analogies?
    a. Change the industry above to match your prospect and/or client.
16. I am working on writing a grant for submission to the Wisconsin Department of Health and Human Services for providing a meal to underserved kids in La Crosse Wi. Could you give me a draft?
17. If I was writing a book to help people use Bing Chat, the target audience is CEO and Business Leaders who have never used an AI. What are 10 prompts in a variety of different scenarios that would work well for them?

Using Google Bard/Gemini AI

Bard is googles public version of its AI. Unlike Bing Chat which does well with real time info. When asked a question like "I am going to Madison". It gives exceptionally generic items about what you could do. Not specific locations or events.

First, go to **https://bard.google.com/** and log in with your personal (not business) google account.
With Bard, we will try prompt 16 from the previous section.

Prompt: *I am working on writing a grant for submission to the Wisconsin Department of Health and Human Services for providing a meal to underserved kids in La Crosse Wi. Could you give me a draft?*
Google Bard:

Title:
Executive Summary:

This grant proposal seeks funding from the Wisconsin Department of Health and Human Services (DHHS) to establish a meal program for underserved children in La Crosse, Wisconsin. The program, titled "Nourishing La Crosse's Youth," aims to address the issue of childhood food insecurity, which affects an estimated 1 in 5 children in Wisconsin. By providing nutritious meals to children in need, the program will promote their physical, mental, and social well-being.

Background:

Childhood food insecurity is a serious problem in Wisconsin. According to the Wisconsin Food Security Survey, 12.2% of Wisconsin households with children were food insecure in 2020. This means that these households were unable to always provide adequate food for their children due to lack of money or resources. The consequences of childhood food insecurity are far-reaching. Children who experience food insecurity are more likely to have health problems, such as anemia, asthma, and obesity. They are also more likely to have behavioral problems and difficulty learning.

Program Description:
The Nourishing La Crosse's Youth program will provide nutritious meals to underserved children in La Crosse, Wisconsin. The program will partner with local schools, community centers, and other organizations to provide meals to children after school, during the summer, and on weekends.
The program will serve a variety of meals, including breakfast, lunch, and dinner. All meals will be prepared with fresh, healthy ingredients and will meet the USDA's nutritional guidelines.

Program Goals:

The goals of the Nourishing La Crosse's Youth program are to:
- Reduce childhood food insecurity in La Crosse
- Improve the nutritional status of underserved children
- Promote the physical, mental, and social well-being of children in need

Evaluation Plan:

The Nourishing La Crosse's Youth program will be evaluated using a variety of methods, including:
- Pre- and post-program surveys to measure changes in children's food security status
- Tracking the number of meals served
- Monitoring children's attendance at meal sites
- Collecting feedback from participants and stakeholders

Budget:

The total cost of the Nourishing La Crosse's Youth program is estimated to be $100,000. This includes the cost of food, labor, and other program expenses.

Conclusion:

The Nourishing La Crosse's Youth program is a critical initiative that will address the issue of childhood food insecurity in La Crosse. By providing nutritious meals to underserved children, the program will promote their physical, mental, and social well-being. We urge the Wisconsin Department of Health and Human Services to support this important program.

This is a good start to grant writing. But more importantly shows the value of AI in creating templates and drafts. The above took less than 2 minutes to create. The more info or detail you would create within it, the more value you would get out of it. Example is, if you had a Funding Opportunity Announcement or Request for proposal. You could paste the text of the FOA or RFP into Bard, and have it written up a draft tailored to that request.

For yourself, look at a few RFP or Quotes and see how Bard can respond to them. Try logging into Bard and using a few of the below prompts. Put Bing Chat and Bard side by side and see which one you like more.

Workshop Time! Copy and Paste the below prompts into Bard, do the same with Bing Chat and other text AI you work with to see which responses you feel are better. Each prompt is highly generic, edit it so it has info about your business, your goal, your product, your problem, your vision. The more you give it, the better the result will be.

Scenario 1: Brainstorming new business ideas

1. Help me brainstorm new business ideas that are aligned with our company's mission and values.
    1. Expand this prompt, paste in your mission and values, tell it what industry you are in and what type of client you want.
2. Generate a list of potential product or service offerings that could address unmet customer needs.
3. Suggest innovative ways to improve our existing products or services.
4. Identify emerging trends in our industry that we can capitalize on.
5. Develop a creative marketing campaign to launch a new product or service.

Scenario 2: Making informed business decisions, make up your own details or paste in your own company details.

6. Analyze a complex business problem and provide me with potential solutions.
7. Evaluate the risks and benefits of different investment opportunities.
8. Conduct a competitive analysis to identify our company's strengths and weaknesses.

9. Generate a market research report to understand customer preferences.
10. Forecast future sales trends to make informed inventory decisions.

Scenario 3: Improving communication and collaboration

11. Draft a persuasive email to a key client.
12. Summarize a lengthy business report in a concise and informative way.
13. Translate a business document from one language to another.
14. Create a presentation that effectively communicates our company's value proposition.
15. Facilitate a productive meeting by providing an objective summary of key points.

Scenario 4: Enhancing personal productivity

16. Consolidate information from multiple sources and provide me with a comprehensive overview.
17. Prioritize my tasks for the day based on their importance and urgency.
18. Schedule appointments and meetings with minimal scheduling conflicts.
19. Keep track of important deadlines and reminders.
20. Provide me with summaries of news articles relevant to my industry.

Highlighting Bard's Advantages over Bing Chat

1. Bard's ability to access and process information from the real world through Google Search gives it a wider range of knowledge than Bing Chat.
2. Bard's ability to generate different creative text formats, like poems, code, scripts, musical pieces, email, letters, etc., makes it more versatile than Bing Chat.
3. Bard's ability to follow instructions and complete requests thoughtfully makes it more reliable than Bing Chat.

4. Bard's ability to answer questions in an informative way, even if they are open ended, challenging, or strange, makes it more helpful than Bing Chat.
5. Bard's ability to translate languages makes it more useful for international business leaders than Bing Chat.

Scenario 1: Generating new business ideas
- What are some innovative ideas that could help my company disrupt the market?
- What are some untapped opportunities in my industry that I could explore?
- What are some emerging trends that I should be aware of?

Scenario 2: Improving operational efficiency
- How can I improve the efficiency of my supply chain?
- How can I automate tasks to free up employee time?
- How can I identify and eliminate bottlenecks in my operations?

Scenario 3: Enhancing customer engagement
- How can I develop a more personalized customer experience?
- How can I use social media to better connect with my customers?
- What are some creative ways to market my products or services?

Scenario 4: Making data-driven decisions
- How can I use data to gain insights into my customers?
- How can I use data to identify areas for improvement in my business?
- How can I use data to make more informed decisions about the future of my company?

Scenario 5: Writing compelling content
- Can you help me write a press release for my new product launch?

- Can you help me write a speech for my upcoming conference?
- Can you help me write a blog post about my company's latest innovation?

Scenario 6: Brainstorming solutions to complex problems
- What are some creative solutions to this problem?
- What are the potential risks and benefits of each solution?
- What is the most effective way to implement this solution?

Scenario 7: Staying up-to-date on industry trends
- What are the latest trends in my industry?
- What are my competitors doing to adapt to these trends?
- How can I ensure that my company stays ahead of the curve?

I would like to highlight some of the things that I do better than Bing Chat:

- I am better at understanding and responding to complex questions.
- I am better at generating creative text formats, like poems, code, scripts, musical pieces, email, letters, etc.
- I am more objective and less likely to express personal opinions or beliefs.

Exploring Image Generation

We delve into the fascinating world of image generation through a comparative analysis of three leading tools: MidJourney, Leonardo, and ChatGPT's Dalle-3. Our objective is to explore their capabilities by generating an image of a complex and detailed nature. We use ChatGPT to construct a highly descriptive prompt, ensuring that the context is limited to the prompt itself for an unbiased comparison.

For our experiment, we tasked ChatGPT 4.0 with developing a prompt for an image: a male warrior with tattoos that emit a blue glow, set against a dystopian, futuristic backdrop. Notably, even with a misspelling in the request ("tatoo"), ChatGPT adeptly interpreted and responded. The generated prompt, unchanged and presented below, served as the input for all three AI tools. Assess their outputs and decide for yourself which tool captures the essence of the prompt most effectively.

PROMPT: *In a futuristic, post-apocalyptic setting, envision a scene where a muscular male warrior stands amidst the ruins of a once-thriving city. He is distinguished by striking, glowing blue tattoos covering his arms and chest, starkly contrasting with his rugged attire. The tattoos, intricate and almost mystical, emit a luminous blue light, casting an eerie glow in the decayed surroundings. The backdrop features crumbled buildings, strewn debris, and rampant vegetation, capturing the desolation of this world. The warrior, with a fierce and determined expression, is battle-ready in this dystopian landscape. The setting is dark and moody, with the warrior's glowing tattoos as a beacon of light and hope amidst the pervasive darkness.*

You can specify the style of the generated image, whether it's cartoonish, character-driven, photorealistic, or anything else. If you're able to articulate your vision, the AI can create it. If you're unsure, engage in a dialogue with the AI, allowing it to guide you in developing the prompt.

It can even ask you questions to refine the details! Test this prompt with your preferred image generator, or experiment with creating your own prompts for a personalized exploration of AI-generated art.

ChatGPT 4.0: GPT came out great and have a video game or cartoon look to them. Many of the examples I see day to day with GPT show this same effect. You likely notice the images in this book have that same effect to them.

With ChatGPT, you can paste in a large section of text and ask it to create a prompt that would create an image.

Midjourney requires Discord to use but has been a tool I have used over the last year. The images are ultra realistic and if I was looking for photographic quality or realism would be one to use based on this test.

These examples ended up looking more like a firefighter calendar photo shoot than intended. After looking at the prompt I can see how the AI thought this what was I wanted.

The detail of the image is impressive when you consider the person in the image doesn't and has never existed. The images above are 100% unique, never before seen and uniquely created for this prompt.

Leonardo.AI was the most realistic but I feel it failed on the glowing tatoo part of the prompt. These images look like someone had blue tatoo ink.

Much like Midjourney, Leonardo took a firefighter calendar photo shoot spin on my request. Review the images and see which one you think is most accurate based on the prompt that was used.

You can also experiment with much smaller prompts. Most image generated prompts I use are only 10 words long and give very good detail with such small prompts.

Image generation is an art in itself and the prompt engineering can get exhausting. It's a skill you will need to practice, refine, and take multiple shots at until it creates a vision you are looking for.

In the last year, image generation is an area I have seen the most improvement in. The images are amazing. In 2022 the big complaint was faces and fingers would never come out correctly. They would have to few or to many fingers, arms and looked goofy. If the images above were on a movie poster you would be hard pressed to know it was Ai generated.

Intermediate AI Usage: ChatGPT

OpenAI's ChatGPT has rapidly progressed in the AI landscape, launching its notable 3.5 version November of 2022 and establishing itself as an essential tool for small businesses. This book concentrates on the most recent advancements and practical uses of ChatGPT. However, the AI field is in a state of constant flux.

A significant change occurred at OpenAI as an unexpected hostile takeover saw CEO, Sam Altman ousted at the height of the its rapid growth in November, who was subsequently hired by Microsoft a few days later. Considering Microsoft's substantial 49% stake in OpenAI and its deep involvement in the company's operations, an Altman move would have had wide reaching impact on the world of AI.

This short coup ended with the board being fired after 95% of employees said they would quit and join Microsoft, who had given them all offers of employment, if Sam Altman wasn't reinstated as CEO. It was a crazy November 2023 to say the least and who knows that futures will unfold with Google Gemi or Meta's AI tools trying to dethrone open AI over the next year.

As of now, ChatGPT 4.0 represents the forefront of AI capabilities for the business world with 4.5 rumors on the horizon. This book aims to guide users in leveraging this advanced technology that we have today while we try to take safe bets about the future.

Getting Started:
Go to https://chat.openai.com/ and create an account, then log in. (YouTube a few videos on creating an account if you can't get it working).
Previous sections you got your feet wet with a few free AI's. To familiarize yourself, take 3.5 or 4.0 through some of the prompts you saw in previous sections of this book and compare the results.

For this section, you should upgrade to 4.0 which is called Pro. Many of the examples such as image creation, custom AI with your own data and advanced writing and answers need the paid for premium version. You are welcome to test the same prompts in 3.5 but will find 4.0 is many multiples better in quality than the free 3.5.
ChatGPT-4.0, with its advanced language models and nuanced understanding, offers several unique capabilities that might not be as developed in Bing Chat or Google Bard. Here are some examples of tasks and prompts that a business person could uniquely leverage with

ChatGPT 4.0:
1. **In-Depth Market Analysis and Trend Prediction:**
    - **Prompt Example:** "Analyze the current trends in the renewable energy market over the past five years and predict the potential developments for the next five years."
2. **Sophisticated Business Strategy Formulation:**
    - **Prompt Example:** "Develop a detailed business strategy for entering the South American e-commerce market, considering local consumer behavior, competition, and regulatory environment."

3. **Complex Problem Solving in Business Scenarios:**
   - **Prompt Example:** "Propose solutions for managing supply chain disruptions in the electronics industry caused by global semiconductor shortages."
4. **Advanced Financial Modeling and Analysis:**
   - **Prompt Example:** "Create a financial model for a startup in the fintech sector, including revenue projections, cost analysis, and break-even analysis."
5. **Creating Detailed Business Plans:**
   - **Prompt Example:** "Draft a comprehensive business plan for a cloud-based SaaS platform targeting small businesses, including market analysis, marketing strategy, operational plan, and financial projections."
6. **Innovative Product Ideation and Development Strategies:**
   - **Prompt Example:** "Generate ideas for innovative smart home products that cater to the needs of urban professionals and outline a development strategy for these products."
7. **Effective Communication and Negotiation Tactics:**
   - **Prompt Example:** "Advise on negotiation tactics for a business deal involving a merger between two major tech companies, focusing on value creation and conflict resolution."
8. **Tailored Marketing and Branding Strategies:**
   - **Prompt Example:** "Develop a unique branding and marketing strategy for an eco-friendly clothing line targeting Gen Z consumers."
9. **Comprehensive Competitor Analysis:**
   - **Prompt Example:** "Conduct a detailed analysis of the top three competitors in the online education sector, focusing on their strengths, weaknesses, and potential strategies for outperforming them."
10. **Customized Legal and Compliance Guidance:**
    - **Prompt Example:** "Provide guidance on compliance with GDPR for a new data analytics service targeting EU markets."

Take some time and try these prompts and compare them to results from the other AI we tested in this.

Other great use cases are:
1. Take an email from a client, paste it into ChatGPT and ask it to write a response. You could even preface it with the type of response or tone you would like.
    a. If it sounds to formal, ask it to rewrite it more casual, or shorter, or say to respond like a friend. If its to casual, ask it to write it as an official notice or letter.
    b. Experiment with the tone, tell it to sound mad, or to sound apologetic, or sound funny.
    c. Critique it, try to think to yourself, why don't I love this letter, what is it missing, what is it including. Then tell the AI that list.
    d. Special note, do not put any confidential or sensitive information in any of these Ai's.
2. Take a quote, RFP in a word format and paste it in. Ask it to write a response.
    a. Any area you feel it is inaccurate in, ask it to correct with the correct information.
3. Reports or Assessments, put the info you have in and ask it to write an assessment.

As a workbook the above are designed for you to go through. Below you will see one of the above prompts and how it plays out within the ChatGPT world. We will pull explaim 5 from above and show you what it looks like to go thorugh.

> **Prompt Example:** "Draft a comprehensive business plan for a cloud-based SaaS platform targeting small businesses, including market analysis, marketing strategy, operational plan, and financial projections."

Step 1: Log into ChatGPT **https://chat.openai.com/**
Step 2: Enter the Prompt into ChatGPT.

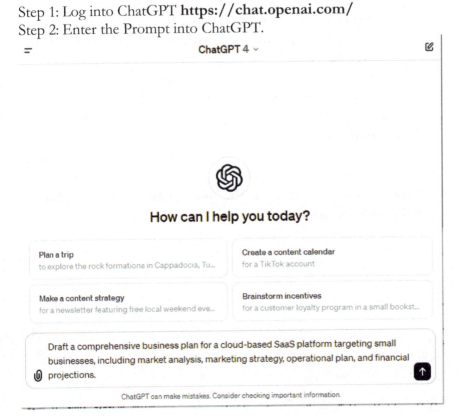

Step 3: Interact with the response. Below is the output ChatGPT gave me from this prompt, it took up many pages as you will see.

Creating a comprehensive business plan for a cloud-based Software as a Service (SaaS) platform targeting small businesses involves several key components. Below is an outline that covers the critical aspects of such a plan:

1. Executive Summary
- **Objective**: *Introduction of the SaaS platform, highlighting its unique selling points and the problems it solves for small businesses.*
- **Vision & Mission**: *Outline the long-term vision and mission of the company.*
- **Key Success Factors**: *Briefly mention what will make the SaaS platform successful.*

2. Company Overview
- **Legal Structure**: *Describe the legal structure of your company (e.g., LLC, Corporation).*
- **History**: *Brief history or background, if any.*
- **Location**: *Headquarters and operational locations.*
- **Team**: *Key team members and their roles.*

3. Market Analysis
- **Industry Overview**: *Current trends and future outlook of the SaaS market.*
- **Target Market**: *Detailed description of the target small business segments.*
- **Competitive Analysis**: *Identify major competitors and their offerings, strengths, and weaknesses.*
- **SWOT Analysis**: *Strengths, Weaknesses, Opportunities, and Threats for your platform.*

4. Product and Services
- **Product Description**: *Detailed description of the SaaS platform, features, and functionalities.*
- **Development Stage**: *Current status of product development.*
- **Intellectual Property**: *Any patents, trademarks, or proprietary technology.*

5. Marketing and Sales Strategy
- **Marketing Plan**: *How you will market your platform (e.g., digital marketing, partnerships, trade shows).*

- **Sales Strategy**: *Sales approach (direct sales, online sales, channel partners).*
- **Pricing Strategy**: *Pricing model (subscription-based, tiered pricing).*
- **Customer Service Plan**: *Support and service strategies for customers.*

6. Operational Plan
   - **Operations**: *Daily operations of the business (customer support, billing, maintenance).*
   - **Suppliers and Partners**: *Any third-party services or partnerships required.*
   - **Technology Infrastructure**: *Cloud infrastructure, software tools, and security measures.*
   - **Human Resources Plan**: *Staffing and organizational structure.*

7. Financial Projections
   - **Revenue Model**: *How the business will make money (subscription fees, add-on services).*
   - **Five-Year Projections**: *Projected income statement, balance sheet, and cash flow.*
   - **Break-Even Analysis**: *When the company expects to become profitable.*
   - **Funding Requirements**: *Any capital needed for start-up and growth, and how it will be used.*

8. Risk Management
   - **Risk Analysis**: *Identify potential risks (market, financial, operational).*
   - **Mitigation Strategies**: *Plans to mitigate identified risks.*

9. Appendices
   - **Supporting Documents**: *Market studies, technical documentation, team resumes.*
   - **Financial Tables and Graphs**: *Detailed financial tables and charts.*

This plan is a blueprint for a cloud-based SaaS platform targeting small businesses. It's important to regularly review and update the business plan to reflect changes in the market and business operations. Also, consider seeking feedback from industry experts and potential customers to refine your plan.

Step 4: This gave you a good overview, in this demo lets have it expand on a component. I am going to enter in the prompt: Please give me more detail on Risk Management (note that is section 8 of the response)

> - **Funding Requirements**: Any capital needed for start-up and growth, and how it will be used.
>
> ### 8. Risk Management
> - **Risk Analysis**: Identify potential risks (market, financial, operational).
> - **Mitigation Strategies**: Plans to mitigate identified risks.
>
> ### 9. Appendices
> - **Supporting Documents**: Market studies, technical documentation, team resumes.
> - **Financial Tables and Graphs**: Detailed financial tables and charts.
>
> This plan is a blueprint for a cloud-based SaaS platform targeting small businesses. It's important to regularly review and update the business plan to reflect changes in the market and business operations. Also, consider seeking feedback from industry experts and potential customers to refine your plan.

> Please expand on documents or responses for what the detail of Risk management might look like.

The Response is another 2 – 3 pages of text. See below:

Certainly! Expanding on the Risk Management section of the business plan for a cloud-based SaaS platform targeting small businesses, it's crucial to identify potential risks, assess their impact, and develop strategies to mitigate them. Here's a detailed breakdown:

Risk Management
1. Risk Identification
- **Market Risks**: *Changes in market trends, new competitors, evolving customer needs, and economic downturns.*
- **Technology Risks**: *Rapid technological changes, cybersecurity threats, data breaches, and software downtime.*
- **Operational Risks**: *Challenges in scaling operations, dependency on third-party vendors, and internal process inefficiencies.*
- **Legal and Compliance Risks**: *Data privacy laws (like GDPR), intellectual property issues, and contract disputes.*

- **Financial Risks**: *Cash flow management, pricing model sustainability, and unexpected expenses.*

2. Risk Assessment
   - **Likelihood of Occurrence**: *Assess how likely each risk is to occur (e.g., high, medium, low).*
   - **Impact Analysis**: *Evaluate the potential impact of each risk on the business (e.g., financial loss, reputation damage).*
   - **Vulnerability Assessment**: *Determine how vulnerable the business is to each identified risk.*

3. Risk Mitigation Strategies
   - **Market Risks**:
     - **Regular Market Research**: *Stay updated with market trends and customer feedback.*
     - **Diversification**: *Expand product features or target markets to reduce dependency on a single market segment.*
   - **Technology Risks**:
     - **Robust IT Infrastructure**: *Invest in reliable and secure cloud infrastructure.*
     - **Regular Software Updates and Backups**: *Ensure software is up-to-date and data is regularly backed up.*
   - **Operational Risks**:
     - **Process Optimization**: *Continuously improve internal processes for efficiency.*
     - **Vendor Management**: *Have contingency plans for vendor-related issues.*
   - **Legal and Compliance Risks**:
     - **Legal Counsel**: *Regular consultation with legal experts to stay compliant with laws.*
     - **Data Security Policies**: *Implement and regularly update data protection policies.*
   - **Financial Risks**:
     - **Cash Flow Management**: *Regular financial monitoring and prudent financial planning.*
     - **Flexible Pricing Strategy**: *Adjust pricing models based on market feedback and financial goals.*

4. Risk Monitoring and Review

- **Regular Reviews**: *Schedule periodic reviews of the risk management plan.*
- **Key Performance Indicators (KPIs)**: *Use KPIs to monitor the effectiveness of risk mitigation strategies.*
- **Feedback Loops**: *Implement mechanisms to receive feedback from employees, customers, and partners on potential risks.*

5. Contingency Plans
- **Emergency Response Plans**: *Have plans in place for immediate response to critical incidents like data breaches.*
- **Business Continuity Planning**: *Strategies for maintaining essential functions during and after a crisis.*
- **Financial Reserves**: *Maintain a reserve fund to manage unforeseen financial challenges.*

6. Documentation and Reporting
- **Risk Management Documentation**: *Maintain detailed records of all risk management activities.*
- **Stakeholder Communication**: *Regularly update stakeholders on risk management efforts and any significant risks.*

Conclusion

Effective risk management is crucial for the stability and growth of a cloud-based SaaS platform. By identifying, assessing, and mitigating risks, and continuously monitoring and adjusting strategies, the business can enhance its resilience and adaptability in a dynamic market environment.

Step 5: Continue to build out your plan/document/presentation until it has the detail you want. In a very short time you can see by repeating the above steps you could get a 40 – 80 page presentation together that has more detail than you ever want to read.

Go thorugh the prompts above and try customizing it to fields of study you are familiar with. It is not perfect; it needs a human to review and guide it. It is exceptionally gifted at creating text and content but needs you to make sure its accurate!

Advanced AI Usage: Custom AI with CustomGPT

ChatGPT has a world of knowledge at its fingertips, it is a genius in most general knowledge but has had trouble understanding context. As of this writing, customGPTs allows you add up to 300 pages worth of custom knowledge to a GPT.

What you need: ChatGPT 4.0 ($20/mo as of the writing of this) and some custom info. For this demo, I am going to create one with 200 pages of HR files from my company from 2018.

!!!WARNING!!! – Do not put sensitive information such as PII, HIPAA or any data you consider confidential.

Lets build a custom AI!
1. To start, log into **https://chat.openai.com/**
2. As of this writing, on the left click "Explore"
3. Click "Create a GPT"

4. Let the AI help you build it. In the lower left, type what you would like this AI to be.

5. It will walk you through creating a bot.

Coulee Tech HR
• Draft

Create | Configure

What would you like to make?

You
I want to make an AI that helps my employee understand company policies and procedures.

GPT Builder
Great, we're creating a GPT that helps employees understand company policies and procedures.

Now, let's give this GPT a name. How about "Policy Guide"? Does that work for you?

You
Lets name it "Coulee Tech HR"

GPT Builder

Here's the profile picture for "Coulee Tech HR." How do you feel about it? Would you like any changes?

6. I ask it to upload file and it says I can. If you don't know how to upload them, you could ask it.

You
I don't know how to upload my files, how many can I do?

GPT Builder
Uploading files is easy! Just click the "Upload File" button, which you can find near the text input area. As for the number of files, you can upload multiple files, but it's best to keep it to a manageable number, especially if they are large or contain complex information. This ensures that I can effectively integrate the content into "Coulee Tech HR." Once you upload the files, I'll incorporate their information into the GPT's behavior. Feel free to start uploading when you're ready!

7. Finish going through the tutorial, it will guide you. Then start testing it out. See below

Coulee Tech HR Bot ⌄

You
My grandmother died, how do I take time off work?

<Beta> Coulee Tech HR Bot
I'm sorry to hear about your loss. According to Coulee Tech's Bereavement Policy, you are entitled to take up to three days off with pay to attend the funeral or make funeral arrangements when a death occurs in your immediate family. This policy specifically includes grandparents in the definition of immediate family, so it applies to your situation.

Please notify your supervisor and HR department as soon as possible to arrange for this leave. In certain circumstances, the company may require verification of the need for the leave. If you need any further assistance or have more questions, please feel free to reach out.

These custom bots add a whole new level to what you can do with an AI. No longer is it a general tool good for general knowledge. In the above example it is answering custom HR questions based on HR policies and procedures as well as informing individuals exactly how to properly do it! If you have ChatGPT Plus, you can go to this link or scan the QR code and try out the Coulee Tech HR bot.

https://chat.openai.com/g/g-DCoRvCL4L-beta-coulee-tech-hr-bot

Spend some time collecting information and building a few custom AI's for yourself. Some idea's:

1. Product Q&A based on products you sell.
    a. Find all the word documents you can and upload them for the different products.
2. Common Sales Objection handling
    a. Start writing down what clients have told you in the past and create a roleplay AI which helps you address those concerns to help your client see the value in your product.
3. Policy and Procedure Doc
4. Use GPT to tell it what industry you are in and what types of custom GPTs could be useful. It will help you help it help you, read that a few times and it makes sense.

IT RFP Generator for Small Business

Assists small businesses in IT RFP creation and answers common IT questions

A useful Custom GPT to try that I built is a small business RFP Generator for Small Business. This tool helps you ask questions from your IT Billing on, what is a 365 charge, while also helping you evaluate IT quotes and is regularly updated by me.

https://chat.openai.com/g/g-ZZLVBvJiu-it-rfp-generator-for-small-business

Driving Non-Profit Efforts with AI

When Aaron and I were talking about this book, he had tons of use cases he had used ChatGPT as president of Fierce Freedom and things he was teaching his clients in Eau Claire. He put together this chapter based on his experience and if you're a non-profit that wants to know other ways to use ChatGPT, Aaron would be a great person to connect with **aaron@coulee.tech**!

Introduction
- Setting the Stage: Challenges Faced by Non-Profits
- The Promise of AI in Addressing Non-Profit Challenges
- Target Audience: Executive Directors, Board Members, and Key Stakeholders

Donor Behavior Predictions
- Leveraging AI for Informed Decision-Making
- Utilizing Machine Learning to Understand Donor Behavior
- Building Donor Segmentation Models
- Predictive Analytics for Improved Fundraising Strategies

Automated Outreach and Campaigns
- Enhancing Engagement and Efficiency
- Implementing AI-Powered Marketing Automation
- Personalization of Communication with AI
- Automating Fundraising Campaigns for Maximized Impact
- Strategies for AI-Enabled Outreach
- Crafting Effective Email Campaigns
- Leveraging AI for social media and Chatbot Engagement

Analyzing the Impact of Charitable Actions with AI
- Data-Driven Accountability and Transparency
- The Significance of Measuring and Reporting Impact
- AI Tools for Assessing Impact
- Building Trust with Donors and Stakeholders
- Evaluating Program Effectiveness

- Real-time Monitoring and Improvement with AI
- Measuring Social and Environmental Impact

Case Studies:
- AI-Driven Insights Transforming Non-Profits

Conclusion
- The Potential of AI to Drive Non-Profit Success
- Encouraging Non-Profit Leaders to Embrace AI
- Practical Recommendations for Implementation
- Paving the Way for AI Integration in Non-Profits

Additional Resources
- List of AI and Non-Profit Collaboration Platforms

Introduction

Non-profit organizations in the United States have long been the backbone of support for local communities, addressing critical issues such as education, healthcare, poverty alleviation, and environmental conservation. These organizations have played a pivotal role in shaping the social fabric of the nation, relying on the generosity of volunteers and donors to make a tangible impact. However, in recent years, non-profits have faced a set of challenges that threaten their ability to fulfill their missions effectively.

Setting the Stage: Challenges Faced by Non-Profits

Non-profit organizations have encountered a series of formidable challenges that have made their work increasingly complex:

- **Declining Volunteer Engagement:** Historically, non-profits have relied on the dedication and hard work of volunteers to support their initiatives. However, a decline in volunteer engagement has left many organizations struggling to execute programs, leading to reduced reach and impact.
- **Decreasing Individual Contributions:** Individual donors have long been a crucial source of funding for non-profits. But in the face of economic uncertainty and changing giving patterns, these organizations have witnessed a steady decline in individual contributions, putting their financial sustainability at risk.

- **Shrinking Corporate Donor Support:** Non-profits have also felt the impact of reduced corporate donor support. As businesses adapt to their own challenges, corporate philanthropy budgets have dwindled, resulting in a loss of significant financial backing for non-profits.

The Promise of AI in Addressing Non-Profit Challenges

In response to these challenges, a glimmer of hope arises in the form of Artificial Intelligence (AI). AI technologies offer the potential to revolutionize the way non-profits operate and achieve their missions. Through data-driven insights, automation, and predictive analytics, AI has the power to help non-profits overcome these hurdles and usher in a new era of effectiveness and efficiency.

AI can assist non-profits in the following key areas:
- **Donor Behavior Predictions:** By analyzing historical donor data and employing predictive analytics, AI can help non-profits gain a deeper understanding of donor behavior. This understanding enables organizations to tailor their fundraising strategies, ultimately increasing donor engagement and contributions.
- **Automated Outreach and Campaigns:** AI-driven marketing automation can enhance non-profit outreach efforts, personalizing communication and streamlining fundraising campaigns. The result is improved efficiency, reaching more potential supporters, and maximizing the impact of these campaigns.
- **Analyzing the Impact of Charitable Actions with AI:** Non-profits can leverage AI to assess the effectiveness of their programs and measure their impact on the community. This not only builds transparency but also helps organizations refine their strategies for greater success.

Target Audience: Executive Directors, Board Members, and Key Stakeholders

This content is crafted for Executive Directors, board members, and other key stakeholders within non-profit organizations in the United States. It can equip these leaders with the knowledge, insights, and practical guidance needed to make informed decisions regarding AI integration. By addressing the specific challenges faced by non-profits and presenting AI as a transformative tool, this content is aimed to empower its readers to adapt, innovate, and continue serving their communities effectively in an evolving landscape. Through AI, non-profits have the potential to drive their efforts to new heights, ensuring a brighter future for both their organizations and the communities they serve.

Donor Behavior Predictions

In today's rapidly evolving landscape of non-profit fundraising, the ability to anticipate and adapt to donor behavior is paramount for success. Leveraging the power of Artificial Intelligence (AI) provides a transformative tool for informed decision-making, enabling non-profit organizations to better understand, engage, and secure the support of their donors. In this section, we dig into how AI can revolutionize the way non-profits approach donor behavior predictions.

Leveraging AI for Informed Decision-Making

AI, specifically through machine learning and predictive analytics, equips non-profits with a data-driven approach to understanding donor behavior. Gone are the days of guesswork and assumptions; AI empowers non-profits to make informed decisions based on concrete insights extracted from their data.

Non-profit organizations can leverage AI for informed decision-making by embracing the following practices:

1. **Data Collection and Storage:** Start by collecting and centralizing all relevant data, including donor information, contributions, communication history, and engagement metrics. This data should be securely stored and easily accessible for analysis.
2. **Data Cleaning and Preprocessing:** Clean and preprocess the data to ensure accuracy and consistency. This step involves removing duplicates, handling missing values, and standardizing data formats.

3. **Machine Learning Models:** Implement machine learning models, which can analyze vast amounts of data to identify patterns, correlations, and trends. These models can provide insights into donor behavior and preferences that may not be apparent through manual analysis.
4. **Predictive Analytics Tools:** Utilize predictive analytics tools to forecast donor behavior, such as predicting when donors are most likely to contribute, which communication channels they prefer, and which campaigns are most likely to resonate with them.
5. **Monitoring and Evaluation:** Continuously monitor and evaluate the performance of AI-driven models and predictive analytics to ensure accuracy and relevance. Adjust and fine-tune the models as needed to improve their predictions over time.
6. **Data-Driven Decision-Making:** Base decisions on the insights generated by AI and predictive analytics. This includes making strategic choices regarding fundraising campaigns, donor outreach, and engagement strategies.

Utilizing Machine Learning to Understand Donor Behavior

Machine learning algorithms analyze historical donor data to identify patterns, preferences, and trends. They can uncover not only what motivates donors to contribute but also when and how they are most likely to engage with an organization. This level of understanding allows non-profits to tailor their outreach efforts and fundraising strategies accordingly.

1) Here are a couple of examples of how non-profit organizations can implement machine learning models to gain insights into donor behavior and preferences:
    a) Donor Retention Prediction:
        i) Challenge: A non-profit is experiencing declining donor retention rates and wants to identify donors at risk of lapsing to take proactive measures.
        ii) Solution: The organization can build a machine learning model that analyzes historical donor data, including giving history, interaction frequency, and engagement levels. The model can predict which donors are most likely to stop contributing in the near future. Non-profit staff can use this information to target these at-risk donors with tailored

communications or incentives to encourage them to continue their support.
2) Personalized Campaign Recommendations:
   a) Challenge: A non-profit is struggling to create effective fundraising campaigns that resonate with its diverse donor base.
   b) Solution: By utilizing machine learning models, the organization can analyze past campaign performance and donor preferences. The model can identify patterns, such as which types of campaigns or messaging are most effective for different segments of donors. As a result, the non-profit can use these insights to personalize campaign recommendations for each donor, increasing the likelihood of engagement and contributions.

In both examples, machine learning models can process vast amounts of donor data to uncover hidden patterns, correlations, and trends that would be difficult to discern through manual analysis. These insights enable non-profits to take targeted and data-driven actions to improve donor retention and tailor their campaigns to individual donor preferences, ultimately leading to more effective and successful fundraising efforts.

Building Donor Segmentation Models

Donor segmentation is essential for personalized engagement. AI enables non-profits to create precise donor segments based on factors such as giving history, demographics, interests, and engagement level. These segmentation models help organizations send the right message to the right donors, significantly increasing the effectiveness of their outreach. To build effective donor segmentation models using AI, non-profits can follow these steps:

1. **Define Segmentation Criteria:** Determine the criteria that will guide segmentation, such as giving history, demographics, geographic location, donor interests, engagement level, and communication preferences.
2. **Data Analysis:** Analyze donor data to categorize donors into distinct segments. This can be done using clustering algorithms that group donors with similar characteristics.
   a. Clustering algorithms are computational methods that automatically group donors into segments or clusters based on similarities in their characteristics, behaviors, or attributes.
      1. In the context of non-profit fundraising, this technique allows organizations to categorize donors into

distinct groups, making it easier to tailor outreach and communication strategies to the specific needs and preferences of each segment. Donor segmentation helps non-profits personalize their interactions with donors, resulting in more effective engagement and fundraising efforts.

2. For example, clustering algorithms might group donors based on criteria such as giving history, demographics, geographic location, interests, engagement levels, or communication preferences. Once donors are segmented, non-profits can create customized communication and fundraising strategies for each segment, increasing the likelihood of donor response and contributions.

3. **Segmentation Validation:** Ensure that the segmentation model is validated and produces meaningful and actionable segments. You can assess the quality of segments by measuring the differences in donor behavior and response rates among the groups.

4. **Personalized Outreach:** Tailor outreach and communication strategies to each segment's preferences and needs. This could involve customizing email content, event invitations, or campaign messages to align with the characteristics of each segment.

5. **Continuous Refinement:** Regularly update and refine donor segmentation models as new data becomes available, allowing for ongoing optimization of engagement strategies.

Predictive Analytics for Improved Fundraising Strategies

The power of AI lies in its predictive capabilities. By utilizing predictive analytics, non-profits can anticipate donor behavior and needs. For instance, they can identify donors at risk of lapsing or predict which donors are most likely to respond to specific campaigns. This insight is invaluable for crafting targeted fundraising strategies that maximize engagement and contributions.

1. Here are a couple of examples of how non-profit organizations can utilize predictive analytics tools to forecast donor behavior and enhance their fundraising efforts:

   a. Optimal Donation Timing:
      1. Challenge: A non-profit wants to maximize its fundraising revenue by sending donation requests at the times when donors are most likely to contribute.

2. Solution: The organization can use predictive analytics to analyze historical donor data and identify patterns in donation timing. By considering factors such as past donation dates, frequency, and engagement levels, the predictive analytics tool can forecast the optimal times to send donation requests to different segments of donors. This results in improved timing of fundraising campaigns, increasing the likelihood of donor contributions.

b. Communication Channel Preferences:
1. Challenge: A non-profit is looking to optimize its communication strategies by delivering messages through donors' preferred channels.
2. Solution: Using predictive analytics, the organization can assess donors' historical response data to different communication channels (e.g., email, social media, direct mail). By analyzing these preferences, the predictive analytics tool can predict which channels are most likely to resonate with individual donors. Non-profit staff can then tailor their outreach efforts to align with these preferences, increasing the likelihood of donor engagement and contributions.

In both examples, predictive analytics tools enable non-profits to anticipate donor behavior, making it possible to optimize the timing of donation requests and tailor communication channels to individual preferences. By leveraging predictive analytics, non-profit organizations can make data-driven decisions that result in more effective fundraising strategies and ultimately greater donor support.

Automated Outreach and Campaigns

In this section, we search into the transformative role of automated outreach and campaigns, specifically tailored for non-profit organizations. By leveraging AI, non-profits can enhance engagement and efficiency, implement marketing automation for personalized communication, and automate fundraising campaigns for maximum impact. The strategies encompass AI-enabled outreach, effective email campaigns, and the utilization of AI in social media and chatbot engagement.

Enhancing Engagement and Efficiency:

Automated outreach offers non-profits the opportunity to significantly enhance engagement and operational efficiency. By leveraging AI-driven tools, organizations can streamline communication processes, ensuring that messages reach the right audience at the right time. This not only boosts donor engagement but also allows staff to focus on high-impact activities, fostering more meaningful connections with supporters.

Implementing AI-Powered Marketing Automation:

AI-powered marketing automation tools enable non-profits to orchestrate and personalize their communication strategies efficiently. These platforms analyze donor data to tailor messages, ensuring that each interaction is relevant and resonates with the recipient. This level of personalization enhances the overall donor experience, potentially increasing response rates and fostering a stronger connection between the non-profit and its supporters.

Imagine you have a magical assistant that helps you with your emails. This assistant, let's call it the "Smart Communicator," looks at the interests and preferences of each person you want to email. It studies what they like, when they prefer to read emails, and even how much they usually contribute. Then, when you're ready to send an email to your supporters, the Smart Communicator steps in. It automatically customizes each email, making it super relevant to each person based on what they know about them. It's like having a personal touch in every message without you having to do all the manual work.

For example, if you have a donor who loves supporting education projects and usually donates during the holiday season, the Smart Communicator will know that. So, when it's time to send out your end-of-year appeal, the assistant would craft a message tailored to their interest in education and highlight the impact of their support during the holiday season. This personalization makes your supporters feel understood and appreciated, increasing the chances they'll engage with your message and continue supporting your cause. It's like having a super-smart helper that makes your communication not just efficient, but also heartfelt and meaningful. That's the power of using AI-powered tools for your marketing and communication needs!

Personalization of Communication with AI:

One of the key advantages of AI in automated outreach is its ability to facilitate personalized communication. Non-profits can utilize AI algorithms to analyze donor preferences, behavior, and engagement history. This information allows organizations to craft highly personalized messages, addressing donors individually and making each communication more impactful and relevant.

Automating Fundraising Campaigns for Maximized Impact:

Automation extends beyond communication to fundraising campaigns. AI can analyze donor behavior to predict optimal times for fundraising appeals, recommend personalized giving amounts, and even identify donors who may be interested in specific initiatives. Automating these aspects of fundraising campaigns ensures that efforts are strategically directed, maximizing impact and response rates.

Let's picture your fundraising efforts as a well-organized party. You, as the host, want to make sure everything is perfect to maximize the enjoyment of your guests (donors). Now, imagine having a super-smart party planner, let's call it the "Fundraiser Wizard."

This wizard doesn't just plan the party; it studies your guests' behaviors and preferences. It knows when they're most likely to be in a party mood (optimal times for appeals), how much they usually contribute (personalized giving amounts), and what specific activities or causes they enjoy the most (identifying interests). Armed with this knowledge, the Fundraiser Wizard takes charge of your fundraising campaigns.

For example, if you have a donor who is passionate about environmental causes, the wizard might suggest reaching out to them when there's a specific initiative related to the environment. It could recommend a personalized donation amount based on their previous contributions and the success of past appeals. By automating these campaign details, the wizard ensures that each fundraising effort is like a perfectly planned surprise tailored to each donor.

This magical automation isn't just about saving you time; it's about strategically directing your efforts to create a big impact. Just like a fantastic party where everyone has a great time, these automated campaigns make sure your donors feel personally connected to your cause. The Fundraiser Wizard takes care of the details, allowing you to focus on the joyous atmosphere of your fundraising "party" and ultimately maximizing the impact and response rates. That's the magic of using AI to automate fundraising campaigns!

Strategies for AI-Enabled Outreach:

AI-enabled outreach strategies involve a comprehensive approach, combining data analytics, targeted messaging, and personalized donor journeys. Non-profits can employ AI to identify and prioritize potential donors, create segmented communication plans, and continuously optimize outreach efforts based on real-time data, ensuring a dynamic and effective approach to engagement.

Imagine you're running a book club, and you want to make sure every member feel engaged and excited about the books you're reading. Now, think of having a super-smart assistant, let's call it the "Engagement Guru," to help you.

This guru doesn't just keep track of who's in the book club; it studies everyone's reading preferences, how often they like to discuss books, and what genres they enjoy the most. Now, when it's time to plan your book club meetings, the Engagement Guru steps in. It automatically identifies who might be most interested in discussing a particular book, creates groups of members with similar tastes (segmented communication plans), and even suggests the best times to send out invites or book recommendations (data analytics).

But here's the real magic: the Engagement Guru doesn't stop there. It keeps learning and adapting. If it notices that certain members prefer shorter books or enjoy more discussion time, it adjusts its strategies for the next meeting (continuously optimizing outreach efforts based on real-time data). This ensures that your book club is always exciting and tailored to what each member loves.

In the world of non-profits, this is similar to employing AI for outreach. The "Engagement Guru" becomes an "AI Outreach Strategist." It helps identify potential donors, creates plans to communicate with them in a way that resonates, and constantly tweaks the approach based on how donors are responding. It's like having a super-smart guide to ensure your outreach efforts are always dynamic, effective, and perfectly tailored to your supporters. That's the power of using AI for outreach strategies!

Crafting Effective Email Campaigns:

Email remains a powerful tool for non-profit communication, and AI can significantly enhance the effectiveness of email campaigns. From subject line optimization to content personalization and delivery timing, AI algorithms can analyze historical data to fine-tune email strategies, increasing open rates, click-through rates, and overall donor engagement.

Leveraging AI for social media and Chatbot Engagement:

Social media and chatbots are valuable channels for non-profit outreach, and AI can play a pivotal role in maximizing their effectiveness. AI algorithms can analyze social media trends, identify optimal posting times, and even facilitate automated interactions through chatbots, providing real-time engagement and support to donors and potential supporters.

Let's imagine you're the host of a big event, like a school fair, where you want to connect with as many people as possible. Now, picture having a magical helper, let's call it the "Social Connector," who knows exactly how to make your event a hit.

This Social Connector isn't just good with people; it understands the trends and patterns of your fairgoers (donors and potential supporters). It knows when most people are likely to attend (optimal posting times on social media), what activities they enjoy the most, and how to make them feel welcome and engaged. Now, let's break down how this Social Connector works:

1. **Analyzing Social Media Trends:**
   - Imagine your school fair as a big party. The Social Connector studies when people are most excited about events like yours. It looks at trends, like which posts get the most likes or shares, and figures out the perfect times to share information about your non-profit on social media.

2. **Identifying Optimal Posting Times:**
   - It's like having a personal assistant who knows the best moments to make announcements. The Social Connector identifies when your potential supporters are most active on social media, ensuring that your posts have the highest chance of being seen and creating a buzz.

3. **Facilitating Automated Interactions through Chatbots:**
   - Now, think of the Social Connector having friendly helpers, or "Chat Ambassadors," at your fair. These ambassadors can answer common questions, provide information, and engage with visitors, making them feel taken care of. In the digital world, these helpers are like chatbots. They provide real-time engagement and support to your online audience, creating a seamless and interactive experience.

In the non-profit world, this Social Connector becomes an "AI Social Media Expert." It helps you understand the best times to share your message, what content resonates the most, and even offers automated support through chatbots. It's like having a magical guide to ensure your online presence is always lively, engaging, and perfectly timed. That's the power of leveraging AI for social media and chatbot engagement!

Analyzing the Impact of Charitable Actions with AI Overview

In this section, we review the transformative role of AI in evaluating and communicating the impact of charitable actions for non-profit organizations. Data-driven accountability and transparency take center stage as we explore the significance of measuring and reporting impact.

We'll examine how AI tools facilitate the assessment of impact, aid in building trust with donors and stakeholders, and contribute to the evaluation of program effectiveness. Real-time monitoring and improvement mechanisms with AI offer dynamic insights, while the exploration of measuring social and environmental impact emphasizes the broader positive outcomes of charitable efforts.

Data-Driven Accountability and Transparency:

Imagine you're running a bake sale to support your cause. Now, picture having a magical calculator, let's call it the "Impact Tracker," that keeps count of every ingredient, every sale, and even the smiles your treats bring. This tracker ensures that every dollar earned is accounted for, offering a transparent and accountable snapshot of your bake sale's impact. In the non-profit realm, AI becomes this "Impact Tracker," allowing organizations to provide a clear and data-driven account of their charitable actions.

The Significance of Measuring and Reporting Impact:

Just like your magical calculator makes sure you know exactly how successful your bake sale was, AI emphasizes the importance of measuring and reporting impact for non-profits. It's like having a report card for your charitable efforts, showcasing not just the quantity but the quality of the positive changes your organization is making in the world.

AI Tools for Assessing Impact:

Imagine your magical calculator evolving into a super-smart "Impact Analyzer." AI tools act as this analyzer, going beyond basic counting to assess the real-world impact of your non-profit's actions. They analyze patterns, trends, and outcomes, providing a deeper understanding of how your organization is making a difference.

Building Trust with Donors and Stakeholders:

Just as your community trusts your bake sale's success because of your transparent tracking, AI helps non-profits build trust with donors and stakeholders. By offering concrete, data-backed evidence of the positive changes achieved, organizations using AI become beacons of trustworthiness and reliability.

Evaluating Program Effectiveness:

Imagine your bake sale expanding into a year-long dessert-making course. Now, think of having a wise mentor, let's call them the "Effectiveness Evaluator," who guides you on how well each session contributes to your ultimate goal. In the non-profit world, this evaluator becomes AI, helping organizations assess the effectiveness of their programs. AI analyzes data in a way that goes beyond just tracking activities—it evaluates how well programs align with goals and where improvements can be made. It's like having a mentor constantly offering insights to make your dessert-making course as impactful as possible.

Real-time Monitoring and Improvement with AI:

Consider running your dessert-making course with an enthusiastic assistant, the "Real-time Refiner," who notices when a recipe isn't quite working and suggests adjustments on the spot. In the non-profit context, AI serves as this real-time refiner, offering immediate insights into how well programs are performing. Whether it's identifying areas for improvement or recognizing what's working exceptionally well, AI enables non-profits to adapt and enhance their initiatives on the fly, ensuring continuous progress and maximum impact.

Measuring Social and Environmental Impact:

Expand your dessert-making course to not only teach baking skills but also instill a love for the environment and community. Now, envision having an eco-conscious mentor, the "Impact Ecologist," who measures not just the success of your desserts but also their positive influence on nature and society. In the non-profit sector, AI becomes this impact ecologist, allowing organizations to measure the broader social and environmental impact of their initiatives. It goes beyond counting dollars raised or people served, incorporating metrics that reflect positive changes in communities and the planet, providing a holistic view of the organization's impact.

Case Studies

AI-Driven Insights Transforming Non-Profits

Real-life examples illustrate the significant impact AI-driven donor behavior predictions can have on non-profit organizations. Here, we showcase organizations that have successfully harnessed AI to transform their fundraising efforts. These case studies provide examples which serve as compelling evidence of AI's transformative potential for non-profit organizations, highlighting the opportunities and benefits that can be realized by those willing to embrace this innovative approach to donor engagement.

Case Study 1: Food Banks and Homeless Services

In a recent Harvard Business Review article titled "How Smart Tech Is Transforming Nonprofits" by Allison Fine and Beth Kanter (published on 12/09/2021 on hbr.org), the transformative impact of smart tech, including AI, on non-profit organizations is explored. One notable case study within the article focuses on Food Banks and Homeless Services.

The integration of AI and smart tech in this context has resulted in several key outcomes:

AI-Powered Donor Behavior Predictions: AI-powered software was utilized to identify potential donors within Food Banks and Homeless Services. This likely involved analyzing past donor behavior to predict future actions, ultimately increasing donor retention. The organization gained the ability to understand donor patterns and preferences, allowing them to tailor their approach for more effective donor engagement.

Optimizing Fundraising Campaign Strategies: The adoption of smart tech, including AI, has revolutionized fundraising efforts for these organizations. AI's capability to process vast amounts of data has been instrumental in optimizing fundraising campaign strategies. This might encompass determining the ideal timing for donor outreach, personalizing messaging to resonate with individual donors, and identifying the most effective communication platforms for engagement.

Impact on Fundraising Revenue and Donor Engagement: The implementation of AI in fundraising campaigns has likely resulted in significant improvements in both fundraising revenue and donor engagement for Food Banks and Homeless Services. By streamlining the donation process and tailoring outreach to donors, these organizations have increased the likelihood of contributions and sustained donor involvement. While specific figures are not provided in the article, the widespread adoption of these technologies suggests that they have positively impacted fundraising outcomes.

Challenges and Successes in AI Integration Process: The article underscores that the adoption of smart tech, including AI, experienced rapid growth during the pandemic. This accelerated integration likely presented challenges related to training staff to use these technologies and adapting to new workflows. However, the successes are evident: AI has not only empowered staff to focus on driving deeper societal changes but, has also facilitated a shift to remote and digital program and service delivery, ensuring these organizations can continue their critical work in a changing landscape.

In summary, AI has played a transformative role within Food Banks and Homeless Services, particularly within the domain of fundraising. By leveraging smart tech and AI, these non-profit organizations have gained a deeper understanding of donors, fine-tuned fundraising strategies, increased revenue, and donor engagement, and successfully navigated the challenges brought about by the pandemic. The integration of AI has proven to be a powerful tool in the non-profit sector, enabling organizations to operate more efficiently and make a greater impact on the communities they serve.

Case Study 2: Save The Children's AI-Powered Fundraising

In the challenging fundraising landscape of 2021, Save The Children Australia sought innovative ways to enhance appeals targeting and increase net revenue. To achieve this, the organization conducted a real-world experiment during their Christmas 2021 appeal, comparing Dataro's AI-powered donor predictions against their traditional RFV segmentation approach. The results showcased the significant impact of AI on donor behavior predictions, campaign optimization, measurable fundraising outcomes, and the overall integration process.

Key points to review and summarize:

Increased Donor Retention with AI-Powered Predictions: Save The Children Australia implemented Dataro's AI-powered donor predictions to enhance their appeals targeting and increase net revenue. The real-world experiment with their Christmas 2021 appeal showed an 18% increase in response rate, indicating that AI-powered predictions contributed to heightened donor retention.

Optimizing Fundraising Campaign Strategies and Messaging: The use of Dataro's AI-powered donor predictions surpassed the traditional RFV (recency, frequency, value) segmentation approach. By integrating Dataro's direct mail appeal propensity scores with their CRM, Save The Children identified donors with the highest likelihood to give. This optimization resulted in a 3.6% increase in net revenue for Dataro's campaign, demonstrating the role of AI in refining fundraising strategies and messaging.

Measurable Impact on Fundraising Revenue and Donor Engagement: The results from Save The Children's experiment showed significant improvements attributable to Dataro's AI-powered predictions. Notably, there was a net revenue increase of over $12,000 with Dataro, and a 14.5% decrease in mailing volume. These outcomes indicate a measurable impact on fundraising revenue, with AI-driven strategies leading to more gifts, higher engagement, and cost savings.

Challenges and Successes in AI Integration Process: While the article doesn't explicitly detail the challenges faced during the AI integration process, it does highlight the successes achieved by Save The Children using Dataro's AI predictions. The organization saved $16,000 across three appeals in the first six months of using Dataro, showcasing the positive outcomes and cost-efficiency achieved through successful AI integration.

In summary, Save The Children's case study highlights the transformative impact of Dataro's AI-powered donor predictions. The organization experienced increased donor retention, optimized fundraising strategies, measurable improvements in revenue and engagement, and demonstrated successes in overcoming challenges during the AI integration process.

Source:
How Save The Children is using AI donor predictions to help build a better world for every child by Dataro.

Conclusion

As we navigate the potential of Artificial Intelligence (AI) in the non-profit landscape, envision this transformative technology as a supportive force, simplifying complex tasks much like a magical assistant orchestrating a successful bake sale. From predicting donor behavior and automating outreach to analyzing and communicating the impact of charitable actions. Embracing AI in the non-profit sector signifies not just adopting a technology but unlocking a new realm of possibilities for a more impactful and successful organizational journey.

The Potential of AI to Drive Non-Profit Success:

Imagine running your non-profit like a well-organized bake sale, but now you have a magical helper, the "Impact Wizard." This wizard, powered by AI, keeps track of everything, showing you not just how much you've earned, but also how effective and impactful your efforts are. It's like having a wise friend who helps you make better decisions for your cause.

Encouraging Non-Profit Leaders to Embrace AI:

Now, think of AI as a friendly mentor, encouraging you to embrace new and smarter ways of running your non-profit. It's not about becoming a tech expert; it's about having a helpful assistant, the "AI Ally," that guides you in making better decisions, understanding your donors, and creating a bigger positive impact. Embracing AI is like welcoming a supportive friend who makes your job easier and your organization more successful.

Practical Recommendations for Implementation:

Implementing AI in your non-profit is like starting a baking class. You don't need to be a master chef; you just need the right recipes. Think of AI as your "Implementation Cookbook." It provides step-by-step guidance, offering practical recommendations tailored for your organization. It's like having a cooking instructor who ensures you follow the right steps to success, making AI integration smooth and effective.

Paving the Way for AI Integration in Non-Profits:

As you consider integrating AI into your non-profit, imagine it as unlocking a treasure chest of possibilities. Picture AI as the "Innovation Navigator," helping you explore new ways to connect with donors, run successful campaigns, and show the true impact of your work. It's like having a trusted guide who paves the way for innovation in your non-profit, opening doors to greater success and making your mission even more powerful. Embracing AI is like discovering a new world of opportunities for your organization.

Additional Resources

Explore the potential of AI with these user-friendly platforms tailored for non-profit success. Each platform brings a unique set of capabilities, simplifying tasks and empowering non-profits to thrive in their missions.

List of AI and Non-Profit Collaboration Platforms

1. **Salesforce Einstein:**
   - Summary: Your personal assistant for managing donors. It helps you understand donor behavior, predicts their preferences, and guides you on the best ways to engage with them.

2. **IBM Watson for Nonprofits:**
   - Summary: A smart friend who helps you understand your data better. It can read and interpret information, making it easier to make decisions and communicate effectively.

3. **Google Cloud AI:**
   - Summary: A toolkit that makes your data work for you. It helps you understand trends, patterns, and insights from your information, like a guide helping you navigate through a sea of data.

4. **Microsoft Azure AI:**
   - Summary: Your personal language expert. It can understand and respond to language, making it great for creating chatbots or interactive experiences without needing to be a tech whiz.

5. **Hootsuite:**
   - Summary: Your social media sidekick. It helps you schedule posts, suggests content your followers will love, and even listens to what people are saying about your non-profit online.

6. **Alteryx:**
   - Summary: A data magician. It blends different data sources seamlessly, helping you create a clear picture of what's happening and making data less confusing.

7. **DonorPerfect:**
   - Summary: Your donor management superhero. It keeps track of your supporters, helps you run effective fundraising campaigns, and ensures you're always in touch with those who believe in your cause.

8. **Kindful:**
   - Summary: Your fundraising partner. It automates tasks, keeps your donor data organized, and helps you focus more on making a difference while it takes care of the details.

10. **ChatGPT by OpenAI:**
    - Summary: Your friendly conversation companion. It can help you create chatbots, automate communication, and engage with people in a natural and friendly way.

These summaries highlight how each platform is like having a helpful friend or assistant specialized in different aspects, making your work easier and more effective without needing to be an AI expert.

Paul Bagniefski: Leveraging AI in Business

Paul Bagniefski

- CEO Mid-City Steel
- Past-Chair La Crosse Chamber of Commerce
- 2023 Distinguished Alumni Award Recipient Western Technical College

At our monthly breakfast gathering at Nutbush, Paul Bagniefski, CEO of Mid-City Steel; Chris Harkness, CEO of Fairway Painting and Sandblasting; and I endeavor to address global challenges and discuss innovative business strategies. These meetings have become a hub for sharing pioneering ideas and advancements.

It was during one such breakfast a year ago that I introduced ChatGPT, a groundbreaking AI product, sparking an engaging discussion on artificial intelligence. In October 2022, just before the launch of ChatGPT, our conversation centered on AI and its role in production automation, coinciding with Paul's exploration of robotic solutions for Mid-City Steel. At that time, ChatGPT represented a significant leap forward in front office automation, a sector previously overlooked.

Over the past year, Paul and I have extensively experimented with ChatGPT, frequently sharing insights through conversations and texts. For Paul, staying abreast of such cutting-edge technologies is crucial; he views them as vital additions to his extensive toolkit.

Paul believes that even if ChatGPT's capabilities were to remain static, it would still be a valuable, albeit minor, asset. However, he is keen on leveraging it to understand its potential evolution and how it can propel his team and company forward.

He anticipates AI transforming industries more rapidly than computers did, highlighting the accessibility and affordability of AI technologies that can be used on various devices without significant investment barriers.

From his experience with the Chamber of Commerce, Paul notes the struggles small businesses face in staffing. In such an economic climate, automation, including AI, can be a game-changer, handling routine, labor-intensive tasks and allowing businesses to focus on their core strengths.

For Paul, ChatGPT has been instrumental in streamlining preparation for Chamber of Commerce meetings, board meetings at Mid-City Steel, and other non-profit endeavors. The AI assists in organizing his ideas into a standardized format, akin to the role of an administrative assistant.

In manufacturing, robotics have been transformative, and similarly, AI has vast potential for small service businesses and front office automation. Paul is exploring ways AI can aid in process mapping and scheduling within his business in 2024.

For client engagement and capability documentation, Paul utilizes AI to simplify technical language, making it comprehensible to those outside the structural steel industry. Similarly, I use AI to enhance my written communication, ensuring it is professional and polished.

The unexpected benefits of AI in social media and Search Engine Optimization are noteworthy, particularly in tailoring content for both algorithmic preferences and general readability.

Reflecting on our collaboration a decade ago, we developed a scheduling system at Mid-City Steel with Coulee Tech. This system, requiring active management, efficiently allocates tasks to employees based on various factors. In 2024, we plan to examine how AI could enhance this system by analyzing historical data to optimize scheduling and identify opportunities for employee cross-training.

A notable AI tool we've used is Read.AI, which joined our meeting as a participant, providing transcription, speech analytics, and summaries with action items. This tool exemplifies the user-friendly nature of modern AI applications.

Paul also discusses AI with his children, comparing it to an advanced version of a 1990s encyclopedia or a powerful Google search. While some in education view AI like ChatGPT as controversial, Paul believes it's imperative for students to become proficient with these technologies, anticipating their future workplaces will demand such skills.

In 2024, Coulee Tech plans to launch monthly workshops for CEOs, an idea born from our breakfast discussions. These workshops aim to enhance executive skills in leveraging technology for business excellence. Paul and I are excited to collaborate in helping businesses in the Coulee Region thrive on national and global scales, empowering them with the necessary tools.

Coach Kowalski Insights: AI in Football and Classroom

Travis Kowalski
Holmen High School Football Coach
Teacher

Coach Kowalski was driving home Last year on the bus from a game up north where he normally has to type up the post-game review. Jason Lulloff, Activities Director was sitting next to him showed him how he can enter some of the key details into an app like ChatGPT, and it writes a tremendous recount of the game as if an NFL writer had joined his team. After a couple edits of anything that is wrong or inaccurate you have a full-page article in less than 5 minutes!

Kowalski ventured into the world of AI tools in sports coaching and teaching started out slow and has evolved into a curiosity of the future his student athletes will be walking into as they graduate. Simple applications like that above and how AI assists in analyzing game strategies and player performance, providing a level of insight that was previously unattainable through the popular film sharing app called Hudl has added more and more statistics and player breakdowns than he would have even dreamed of 16 years ago when he started coaching.

I find myself intrigued by the precision and efficiency that AI brings to sports analytics, a field traditionally reliant on human observation and intuition.

Travis is not just a coach; he spends a large portion of his professional life as a teacher at Holmen High School. As an educator he was first caution about the AI with unknown impacts the school district still wrestles with. As he pilots a few safe ways he can engage with students highlighting its role in personalizing learning experiences for students.

He shares examples of AI applications that help students in areas where they struggle, adapting to their learning pace and style. This resonates with my belief in the potential of AI to revolutionize education by catering to individual learning needs.

A significant part of our conversation revolves around the ethical implications and challenges of using AI. We ponder the balance between technological advancement and maintaining human elements in teaching and coaching. Travis expresses his concerns about over-reliance on technology, fearing it might overshadow the human touch that is crucial in education and sports. I echo his concerns, emphasizing the need for a balanced approach where AI complements rather than replaces human interaction.

Kowalski also touches upon the use of AI for administrative tasks in education, such as scheduling and communication with parents. He finds this aspect particularly beneficial, as it frees up more time for him to focus on teaching and personal time investments in his students.

Educators work tremendously long hours during the school year and finding ways to reduce back-office work lets those educators reinvest in the real reason they are there, which is the students.

One area of particular interest to me was when Coach Kowalski started sharing how injury and concussion reduction was a huge part of the football landscape now and envisages a scenario where AI could offer more advanced analytics in sports, possibly even predicting injury risks and optimizing training regimens to reduce them.

My son, who plays for Holmen High School under Coach Kowalski suffered a broken hand this year. Kowalski talks about how his helmet providers has new sensors that can get embedded into the helmets which registers every hit is transmitted to medical staff live on the side lines where they can pull a student that may show no symptoms entirely based on registration within the helmet of a hit.

This was technology I thought only the NFL had! To which Travis shared he has access to more sideline technology than the NFL because they are not allowed to use most of what he has access to!

In education, he foresees AI playing a significant role in creating more engaging and interactive learning environments.

Towards the end of our conversation, Travis asks for my perspective on the future of AI in these domains. I share my optimism, envisioning a future where AI seamlessly integrates into both education and sports, enhancing the roles of teachers and coaches. However, he also cautions against becoming too dependent on technology, stressing the importance of maintaining a human-centered approach in both fields.

Harnessing AI's Power in Real Estate: A Conversation with Keagan Walz

Keagan Walz
- Realtor at The Siewert Group
- Co-Founder/Co-Host of Pay It Forward Podcast
  Over a million views in its 1st year!
  https://linktr.ee/payitforwardpodcast

Jasper AI: Generating real estate listings and other content.
ChatGPT: Content creation and scriptwriting.
Opus Clip: AI-generated video editing.
CapCut: Video editing capabilities.
Leonardo.ai: AI-generated images.
Ask the Public: Identifying trending questions
vidIQ: Utilized for identifying daily topics and analyzing competition, especially useful in content creation for platforms like YouTube.

As I sit down with Keagan, a seasoned user of artificial intelligence in his business ventures, I'm eager to delve into his experiences and insights. This conversation is not just about exploring the capabilities of AI but understanding its tangible impact on the day-to-day operations of a business leader.

Revolutionizing Real Estate with AI Keagan's journey with AI began in the realm of real estate. Starting out with tools like Jasper AI and Chat GPT have transformed the way he approaches property listings.

What would take 30 – 60 minutes in typing up an average listing for his clients. He uses Jasper, gives the raw details of the house and gets a great template that only needs minor tweeks to be perfect for his clients! The speed and efficiency brought about by AI in creating compelling descriptions are nothing short of revolutionary.

As time has moved on he finds the AI is getting better and better requiring less time in editing to the point where some of them have required no editing. This comes from both the improvement in AI as well as his increased experience in prompt engineering to he knows what to tell the AI and how to word it for the outcome he is looking for.

It's a vivid example for CEOs of smaller companies: AI is not a distant, complex technology but a practical tool that can offer immediate benefits that get significantly better the more experience you get.

AI's Role in Refining Sales Strategies
Our discussion naturally progresses to the application of AI in sales. Keagan illustrates the effectiveness of AI-generated scripts that resonate with his own voice and style. It helps him negotiate for his clients by role playing objections and getting answers that help his clients secure a more favorable outcome. It's about crafting a narrative that doesn't just sell but connects. This personalized approach in AI scripting is a critical element in overcoming sales objections and engaging clients more effectively.

Venturing into AI-Driven Video Editing

As Keagan navigates the dynamic world of AI in video editing, his involvement in the successful "Pay It Forward" podcast has propelled him to discover innovative ways to enhance the channel's reach.

Discussing the forefront of video editing technology, he points to advanced tools like Opus Clip and CapCut, along with his latest interest in Leonardo.ai for image creation. While video editing is still catching up to the strides made in conversational AI and image generation, these tools have significantly reduced the time spent on editing and refining content. However, there's still room for growth in terms of efficiency comparable to text or image AI tools.

One notable feature Keagan highlights is the ability of these tools to evaluate the social engagement potential of specific video segments. This insight has been instrumental in optimizing his content, contributing to the remarkable achievement of over a million views on several clips in just the first year. Leonardo.ai, in particular, has been a game-changer in creating compelling thumbnails. These tools are not just about saving time; they are redefining the landscape of AI-driven content creation, especially in the realms of video and image generation.

Content Creation with GPT: A Game Changer

Keagan emphasizes the strategic use of GPT in content creation. He underscores the importance of well-thought-out prompts to extract the most creative and relevant output from AI. This approach, he notes, has been instrumental in overcoming creative blocks and generating innovative content ideas.

Envisioning the Future of AI in Creative Processes

As our conversation concludes, we focus on the future of AI in content creation and social media management. Keagan voices a need for more intuitive and user-friendly AI tools that can integrate more seamlessly into creative processes. The potential for AI to become a more accessible and effective tool for business leaders, especially in small and medium enterprises, is immense.

Through this dialogue with Keagan, I am reminded of the dynamic and ever-evolving nature of AI. It's a journey of continuous learning and adaptation, but one that promises to redefine the landscape of business operations and creativity. I am thankful for Keagan sharing his insight and he will inspire readers to embrace AI in their own business endeavors, unlocking new potentials and opportunities.

Coach Yash Insights: AI in Everyday Life and Education

Tom Yashinsky (aka Coach Yash)
Onalaska High School Football Coach & Health Teacher

Coach Yash, Onalaska high school teacher and coach, is preparing for his day. He's using ChatGPT to generate discussion questions to engage his students for his health class. The tool effortlessly crafts insightful queries that would prompt critical thinking among his students allowing him more time to connect with his students before class.

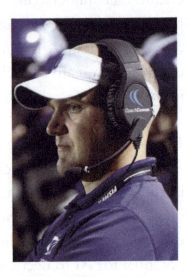

Tom then transitions to creating a letter of recommendation. The AI's fluency in generating formal documents is highlighted, showcasing its versatility. He reflects on the time saved and the improved quality of his work, setting the stage for a broader discussion on AI's impact in the educational sphere.

As Tom prepares for a meeting, he uses beautiful.ai to create an engaging slide presentation. The AI's ability to transform mundane data into visually appealing formats is emphasized, illustrating its potential to enhance communication, and learning experiences.

Revolutionizing Education with AI
Rod Holum, CEO of Coulee Tech, had the opportunity to interview Coach Yashinsky to see how a local leader uses AI. It was interesting to see many unique uses he has and how he empowers these tools to better help him connect with his students.

We delved into the transformative role of ChatGPT in his professional lives. Tom gave several unique use cases he has used them over the last year. One instance, Tom used ChatGPT to write code for a program that processes sports streams, showcasing AI's versatility beyond traditional educational uses. This gave Tom access to tools that were well beyond his normal ability as an educator.

Tom adds his experience of real-time language translation of chats from German to English, with a service he was using that underscoring AI's role as a bridge in global communication. I asked if such tech could be used with students assisting non-English speaking and foreign exchange students, painting a picture of an inclusive educational environment fostered by AI. He cited other services the school has access to, but it could be a valuable secondary resource.

We changed to ponder the evolution of AI in education. We muse on its omnipresence in the future and its role in verifying the authenticity of essays and homework. It has caused some issues with educators, but he believes most teachers have adapted well, from expanded use of plagiarism and AI checkers, as well as common sense steps of knowing your students and if they use words and styles well beyond their capability it can run some red flags.

Some educators for personal use have the notion of AI as a cheating tool, others frame it instead as a time-saving aid that allows educators and students to focus on critical thinking and creativity, but both must be done with honestly and agreement between students and educators on a case by case basis.

The Dawn of a New Era in Education
Many educators are starting to see the time-saving tools in enhancing productivity and fostering human interaction, a crucial element often overshadowed by technology.

We then venture into the future of AI, with a nod to OpenAI's CoPilot integrating into Microsoft's suite. I am very excited about this development, hinting at a future where AI's potential is fully realized in everyday tools.

We closed out our conversation pondering the ethical considerations, with Tom opinion leaning that AI, when used responsibly, is more of an aid than a cheat. I suggest innovative methods to integrate AI without compromising academic integrity are great viewpoints as we navigate these new tools with schools. A point we must continue to contemplate the delicate balance between technology and traditional educational values.

Loree Coulthard: HR and Healthcare

Loree Coulthard

Human Resource Coordinator – Arbor Place Inc
Menomonie Wi

Loree Coulthard, HR Coordinator at Arbor Place Inc., was an ideal interviewee for my book on the burgeoning role of AI in modern businesses. Her dynamic approach and innovative spirit perfectly encapsulated the way small and medium-sized enterprises are harnessing AI to transform their operations.

As we began our discussion, I proposed starting with the foundational aspects of AI in HR, aiming to illuminate its role and potential impact for our readers. Loree, with an expression blending experience and anticipation, shared how she initially experimented with AI, using it for tasks such as email drafting of acceptance and offer letters and job description creation.

This initial step into AI proved to be a significant move towards enhancing efficiency and saving time. At this point, almost every professional communication has some level of AI involvement in its creation. As a medical organization and HR dealing with HIPAA, Personal Health Information (PHI), and Personal Identifiable Information (PII) this has created unique work arounds.

These AIs are outside of the controlled data, which means you must put filler data in places where PII/PHI might go. Loree has found an easy work around for this is to put place holders. IF she was writing an offer letter to Rod Holum. Instead of putting that persons name in she prompts it "Write an offer letter to <first and last name> for this position". Then copy and paste it into the actual offer and edit it.
Our conversation naturally evolved to explore the more nuanced applications of AI. Loree recounted a personal experience where she turned to Chat GPT for support during a difficult personal time, noting the unique ability of AI to provide not only factual responses but also ethical guidance and emotional comfort.

Curious about the practical impact of AI in professional settings, I inquired about its influence on more intricate tasks. Loree highlighted the use of AI in developing comprehensive internship programs and policy documents, emphasizing AI's role as an enhancement to human capabilities rather than a replacement.

Loree is the subject matter expert, but the AI creates a number of boilerplate templates that she can quickly customize for her use. This replaces the labor intensive portions of program creation and allows her to focus on customization of it to meet her unique needs in Arbor Place, Inc.

I delved into the challenges and limitations associated with AI, a topic Loree approached with openness and insight. She stressed the importance of understanding and validating the information provided by AI, particularly when dealing with sensitive data. Tips and tricks like identifying the phi/pii data and simply creating place holders for that data allow her to work with both.

As our talk shifted to the future possibilities of AI, Loree shared her plans to utilize AI in areas such as grant writing and large-scale building projects. Much like the intern program or hr processes. AI can be used to create the boilerplate grand with generalized info then grant writers can customize that data to perfectly match the grant request. This improvement could allow them to apply for twice as many grants as they had in the past.

She also mentioned the advantages of using tools like Enlightened for managing IT tickets and PCs, showcasing the versatility of AI applications. Which is a client facing IT tool Coulee Tech developed for its clients and is starting to incorporate these AI features for summarization of client environments for decision makers.

When the conversation turned to the topic of custom AI solutions, Loree expressed her keen interest in how custom GPTs and APIs could provide tailored solutions for Arbor Place. She recognized the significant potential of AI in managing complex data and producing customized summaries. This topic is one we dive into in this book in other chapters.

Concluding our discussion, I was struck by the profound impact AI has had on businesses like Arbor Place. Loree's experiences, spanning from personal support to intricate business applications, painted a vivid picture of the AI revolution in the realm of small and medium enterprises. This year Loree is on the cutting edge of AI use compared to her peers, our hope is sharing these use cases will help make this type of AI use far more common in both medical and hr groups.

Made in the USA
Monee, IL
31 January 2024